Winding Brook Stories

by

Ron Ridenour

Cover and photos by Jette Salling.
This is the Winding Brook flowing by
Denmark's Tvind school center and a
Zimbabwe artist's sculpture.

Jette Salling has now illustrated

three of Ron's books.

Another kind of education!

"The world is our classroom." - Justas, Communicator-Recruiter

"I usually feel somewhat outside modernity, but with this school community, I feel less so. I even began writing again, stream of consciousness to help me understand today's world." - Francesco, Student Teacher

"I was reflecting too much on human beings and not acting enough with humans. I was torn between wanting to go further with academia, becoming a professor of philosophy, or being myself. There were too many rules in academia...A friend showed me an article about a traveling college education somewhere in Denmark. I looked it up and got hooked on Tvind and the Necessary Teacher Training schooling." - Guenda, Student

"Thanks to the businessman's Rotary Club, I joined the anti-capitalist Teachers Group." - Anna, Teacher

"I see this school community as a center for humanity. I hope we can help radicalize many young people to fight to end poverty. We are not in the vanguard of starting a revolution but when it does start, I hope we will be one of many oases for people fighting against capitalism and imperialism." - Gert, Teacher

"Anyone's first association with those involved with Tvind ... will give you a whole load of stuff to read and attempt to sort through, including accusations that the founders of the organization are cult leaders and criminals ... My own experience has been that some of the most knowledgeable, caring and shining souls I have ever met have been Tvind founders, members of the Teachers Group." - David Rovics, world touring troubadour, often sings for Tvind/Teachers Group arrangements.

Fighting with the poor to end poverty and wars!

Published by
Literary Vagabond Books
Los Angeles • Osaka
literaryvagabond.com

Winding Brook Stories

Print Book ISBN #978-1-70623-644-3

Cover design by Jette Salling.

WINDING BROOK STORIES

Table of Contents

PREFACE

This series of teacher-student stories, interspersed with journalistic materials and writing, is aimed at showing how thousands of mainly white Europeans and Americans from both continents together with millions of Africans and peoples from India struggle to eradicate, or greatly reduce, poverty by "fighting with the poor". They do so out of "solidarity humanism" by using a unique and radical schooling – "another kind of school: learning by doing" – and through concrete development projects for sustainable agriculture and environment; community development; and improving the health of people by preventing-treating HIV and AIDS, tuberculosis, malaria and other epidemics.

What is unusual and noteworthy about these radicals, in contrast to most Western radical-revolutionary-communist groups and political parties, is that they have survived, are even growing and making progress, and doing so despite much political opposition, including by media not only in Denmark but also in the US and elsewhere.

On July 1, 1970, a team of ten young teachers and 40 students started the DRH (Danish letters for The Traveling Folk High School). Under the leadership then of Mogens Amdi Petersen, they hired the Rantzausminde Efterskole (literally "afterschool", the equivalent of the 10th grade) on the Danish island of Fyn. They renovated five buses to travel back and forth to India (Nepal) – a seven month hands-on, practical-theoretical educational-solidarity trip.

Students studied the background and history of the countries they were to visit. Once returning they traveled Denmark to learn its reality and bring to Danes what they had learned in India. Later on, they elaborated their studies so graduates of 9/10 to 24-month DRH studies could become Development Instructors (DI). Since then they have brought their knowledge and practical solidarity to people in many countries. Today, the curriculum includes learning English well, at least some Danish, global affairs, political science, international and economic development.

Many of these educational pioneers started the "Teachers Group" (TG). They took ideas from several radical and revolutionary groups seeking an end to capitalism's greedy economic system, an end to its exploitation and oppression of workers and others, an end to their wars for profit. They supported liberation struggles against colonialism, especially in Africa.

Teachers Group made a life style commitment as a family of teacher-revolutionary comrades that includes living with a *common economy, common time and common distribution*. All earnings are shared. Each individual takes a like sum for personal expenses, which varies depending upon needs, and the larger portion pays the common bills, and helps finance agreed-upon projects to advance their ideas. Even rarer for radicals was/is their firm commitment from the get-go not to imbibe alcohol or any drugs, including marijuana, neither on the premises nor during their educational travels, and that means all teachers and all students. They learned that alcohol and drugs impair people's abilities to work smoothly together, and get in the way of effective work habits.

When accepted as part of TG, one decides to hold together through thick and thin. The minimum commitment asked for is five years. Many make a decision for life. If a member decides to leave, so be it, although in the early days there was substantial pressure to fulfill the time commitment made.

TG's first mentor was the revolutionary Ukrainian pedagogue Anton Makarenko. Makarenko, together with colleagues, ran a farm-school for difficult children, rebels without a cause. The teachers managed to turn most of the juveniles away from a destructive trajectory by combining hard work and disciplined education. Gradually the youth participated productively. The fields were cultivated for self-sufficiency, and craftsmen were hired to train the youth to build workshops. Makarenko often read aloud the youth. He later wrote several books. "The Road to Life" is best known. He argued that humans are both natural and cultural beings, and that we can transcend our nature by consciously taking decisions and actions on moral and social-philosophical issues.

The Teachers Group soon moved to an empty hotel on another island, Fanø, and DRH was expanded. Three teams were sent off in 1972, and four teams each year thereafter. In their view, traveling is an education in itself, even an art that "takes your mind and soul to new heights, it confounds you in the process, and it lets you contemplate life and how people live it."

In August 1972, TG bought a country house with 13 hectares of land (half in pine trees) near a little rural town, Ulfborg, in west Jutland. The farm garden was called Tvind (Its history comes later).

TG members developed a new four-year educational program (sometimes three years), DNS (Danish letters for The Necessary Teacher Training College). They called this education "necessary", in order to adequately meet the "times are a changing" – bringing more relevant knowledge to youth, help mobilize them to meet the new demands and challenges: reduce inequality and poverty, eliminate racism and wars. Not only a political statement then but also now.

In September, the first seminar started to educate students to be primary school teachers (later on to become teachers for secondary classes and beyond). At first, the Ministry of Education approved DNS as a pilot scheme in which 80 students were to complete the seminar, in 1972-76. The first teachers were DRH "veterans".

Denmark has a uniquely liberal law that grants state economic support to what is called, "high schools" – privately run free schools, which individuals, groups or organizations can create by meeting minimal rules. These schools are for students who have finished the required nine years of government "folk" schools. This concept began in 1844 as an alternative to traditional government schools. Its founder, N.F.S. Grundtvig, was a theologian-philosopher, poet-politician, who also influenced the first constitution enacted in 1848.

Teachers Group developed other educational programs for many types of students, including those with "special needs". At the Tvind campus today, one of them is PTG (Practical-Theoretical Basic Education), which is a boarding school for especially "difficult" youth mixed with well-functioning youth. PTG employs educated teacher-caretakers, plus DNS student assistants, who also get help from the well-functioning youth. Municipalities send special needy youth to this boarding school.

In addition, there is a Day School for children who otherwise would be in the regular primary-secondary classes but who need special attention. Sometimes there is one or two teachers and teacher assistants per pupil. Many of the children have been abused or abandoned by parents or by inadequate foster parents. Here they learn what they otherwise would in "folk schools" plus a bit of Teachers Group's solidarity views on humanity.

Tvind also has a special "residential offer" for adults with social-physical-psychological difficulties. These programs include specially designed care and curriculum for each individual.

At the root of Teachers Group education is teaching that solidarity and peace are essential for all human beings. It is no wonder then that The Establishment soon characterized the TG as subversives who must be stopped. There have been many criticisms of their methods (to be presented further on) even a law prohibiting any state funding, which the Danish Supreme Court overturned; and a court case claiming that its original leaders had embezzled money from some projects and placed funds in others, and had evaded paying taxes. All but one of those charged were found not guilty. The government later appealed the court's decision after the absolved defendants returned to where they were living, most of them in Zimbabwe.

Despite the fact that the government does not support the DNS and DRH more politically oriented schooling, and propagandizes against the Teachers Group, between 30 and 50 municipalities (around half the nation) send "clients", "patients" to these other schools simply because Tvind (and sister school Lindersvold) have become good at these specialties.

TG did not organize a political party nor embrace a particular ideology with leading figures – not Marx-Engels, Lenin, Trotsky, Stalin, Mao, Hoxha,

Tito, Ho Chi Minh, Pol Pot, Fidel or Che. Albeit, TG's DRH and DNS educational programs do incorporate some Marxist teachings within contemporary contexts, and they do advocate an economy based on cooperation and equality.

Some revolutionaries criticize TG, and organizations where they work, for seeking government aid to help finance projects that they wish to support, and they raise funds from corporate foundations and NGOs to which some leftists snub their noses. (More on this later on.)

What no one can condemn them for, not even The Establishment and its mass media, is Tvindkraft (Tvind Power). Built between 1975-8, the wind turbine is 54 meters tall with a 54 meter wingspread, at the time the world's largest. Four hundred people began the construction. Through the years several thousands participated, and around 100,000 people visited Tvind to watch the process. When the mill was completed, it had only cost the equivalent of $1 million in today's value – paid for out of Tvind teachers' salaries. It still operates today and provides all Tvind's electric needs.

Tvindkraft, at the time built 1999 it was the world's largest windmill. Photo by Jette Salling

The Teacher's Group offered the designs and ideas to anyone, but the state didn't want them because it was committed to going with nuclear energy. Nevertheless, the Danish people soon rejected this idea, in part because Tvind showed that windmill energy was possible, cheaper and much better for the environment. Tvindkraft is the basis for all of Denmark's famous windmills. It took the largest windmill company, Vestas, 20 years to make a windmill as powerful as Tvindkraft. (US American political folk singer-writer David Rovics wrote a song about this: https://www.tvindkraft.dk/en/david-rovic-the-biggest-windmill-in-the-world.html)

In 1977, TG started UFF-Humana (Development Aid People to People) to collect, sort and sell used clothing, in order to finance various projects. This was the beginning of what became the Humana People to People (HPP) organization. The first aid was given to Zimbabwean refugees in camps in Mozambique and the first development projects were established in Zimbabwe in 1980. Today, Humana People to People has 30 national associations working with around 8000 employees in 45 countries of Europe, the US, Latin America, Africa and India. There are around 1000 long-term sustainable development programs, which reach between eight and 14 million people yearly.

The Teacher's Group has grown to 3000 members. There is no one leader rather a council of Teacher's Groups at each facility where they work. Teachers Group practices the principle of not making decisions based on polls. Discussions take place until everyone agrees. This consensus ruling has sometimes resulted in long and conflict-ridden meetings until the most "articulate" and most enduring persons win. That phenomenon was typical of many left groups but is less so today.

In Denmark alone the schools that Tvind started have numbered in the scores. Today, Tvind school community is the only Danish school that teaches TG's pearl program, DNS. An associate school, The Travelling Folk High School in rural Lindersvold, teaches two programs of 10 and 24 months. In nearly 50 years now, schools where members of TG teach have graduated around 1000 DNS teachers and 45,000 students in all, including those with special needs.

Traveling Folk High School courses are also offered at the One World Center in Michigan, at Dowagiac where the Pokagon band of the Potawtomi people are headquartered; One World Institute in Hornsjoe Norway; College for International Co-operation and Development in Patrington England; and Richmond Vale Academy in Eastern Caribbean (St. Vincent and the Grenadines).

African DNS schools use the basic program that Tvind school community created, and adapted it to their own local/national needs. The traveling part of the education is limited to other parts of their own country or to an African neighbor.

I have read and skimmed through the two basic African DNS textbooks. The older one designed for three African countries is 400 pages, and the newer Mozambique One World University textbook is 680 pages. Much of the material is taken from Tvind's newest Denmark edition (2011) of 480 pages. It is not just a matter of the amount of words, of course, but the curriculum, the worldview is comparable to all the schools.

Since 1993, Humana People to People has been at the forefront of educating African and Indian teachers, who commit themselves to work in public primary schools, sometimes that they help construct. More than 42,000 teachers have been educated in Mozambique, Angola, Malawi, Guinea Bissau, Zambia, D. R. Congo and India. The teacher training colleges have DNS programs spanning from one to three years, and all except those in India are boarding schools.

In 1998, One World University was started in Mozambique and now teaches DNS in all 12 provinces. This university is recognized, and partially financed by the government. OWU has graduated around 1000 teachers with a bachelor or masters degree. DNS schooling exists in 14 colleges in Angola with some 6000 teacher graduated. Malawi is launching six DNS colleges and has graduated around 2000 teachers. Guinea Bissau is constructing seven colleges with a goal of graduating 840 primary school teachers annually. Zambia is committed to building eight schools; one is now operating. Congo Democratic Republic has one DNS college with scores planned. There are DNS schools in 18 locations in three states of India.

I spent three weeks at Denmark Teacher Group-run DNS and DRH schools observing some classes, interviewing many people, assisting in the kitchen and garden, and then many weeks reading about what they do, their history, and what their critics say about them. My viewpoint is that these people are dedicated to changing the world where poverty and wars no longer exist. In so doing, they have made many good choices and some I would not. Readers who know my writings probably can say I am too idealistic. I hope that all readers can count on my non-neutral objectivity.

CHAPTER ONE
Communicator-Recruiter Justas

Justinas (Justas) Volungevicius. Lithuanian student
recent graduate now in Teachers Group

"The world is our classroom"

Justas picked me up at the train station. We rode in an elder Tvind car to the campus where I would live for eight days preparing for this series. I hoped this would be a positive story for me – being with people who actually embody the vision of liberation, and fight with the oppressed, jointly struggling to empower their lives. This would be a rarity for me as nearly all my writings reflect the evils and profiteering humans inflict upon one another and the planet.

Justinas Volungevicius (Justas for short and as play on words indicating that justice is sought) came to Tvind when 16. After six years of going through two educations, he is now a Tvind administrative-communication worker. As such, he does media and recruiting work for the various schooling processes. When The Necessary Teacher Training College class of 2017 (DNS 17) started, Justas assisted as a media aid advisor.

There were some criticisms about a few aspects of the program presented. Some thought that parts were outdated. They also wanted to improve residential conditions, and the garden. This resulted in a name change of the residential building where they live and where I would stay: "Radical October 17".

Justas explains. "Radical October came about because of DNS teams expressing the need and the wish to be part of making the school better. DNS17 stepped in the middle of this process. It was not a rebellion against an 'establishment' rather that students and teachers discuss how to improve the school. Everyone got involved out of a longing to be part of making the place and the schooling better, learning in the process what it actually takes to run the school together.

"When I discuss enrollment with potential students, I ask: 'Are you ready to face challenges? Because our program is by far from perfect. But if you choose to take ownership and responsibility of what we have and are part of creating what is missing or not good enough, I guarantee you will learn a lot.'"

They brought their critical ideas to the school's weekly meeting with two teachers (also from Lithuania), and the headmaster Annica Mårtinsson. Born in Sweden, she came to Tvind a quarter-century ago to take its schooling and join the Teachers Group (TG). The staff agreed to implement the students' ideas even though this would set back the three-year schedule by one month. The work was done in October and thereby the new name for the building.

Justas recorded some of this work for the DNS website.

https://www.dns-tvind.dk/radical-teachers/

DNS17 students had invited me to follow their study period this week, and to offer a half-day's "course" on Cuba's revolution and US subversion. These eight students come from half-a-dozen lands: three from Italy, two Portuguese, two Lithuanians, and one from Hungary.

I could tell that the building had recently been renovated, and it is kept clean. The rooms are usually for two students. I was offered a room to myself. There is enough space for two single beds, writing desk and chair, closet, and some bookshelves. Heat comes through a radiator furnished by wood cut from their forest and from wind.

Before Justas and I had discussion time, another young member of TG, also from Lithuania, Nadezda Jevdokimova, was my guide for the day. We went through the campus six schools and the residential areas, workshops and maintenance – 30 buildings in all.

Gateway to the Tvind school campus designed by architect Jan Utzon.

The school community currently have around 100 students-boarders, and 30-40 teachers, teacher assistants, administrative and maintenance workers. Each of their schools has its own leadership, board of directors, financing and book accounting. Now there are four DNS classes (with start dates 2016-19), the PTG youth school (Practical-Theoretical Basic Education), a Day School for especially needy youth in which they get some education and are boarded, and three "villas" where 15 adults can be cared for. At PTG and the Day School, a special program is designed for each student, and another criterion is made for adults at the "villas". Every student is offered a computer. Each school has its own library. Tvind has its own printing press for posters, placards, brochures. Their hardcover glossy text and culture books are printed elsewhere. All who are able physically and/or mentally to travel out of Denmark for one to three week annual trips can do so in groups with teachers. This is paid for with government funding. Municipality payment for students and adults needing special care helps finance the studies of DNS and other well-functioning students through their wages as many work as assistants with the boarders.

Nadezda introduced me to "The President", 51 year-old man, who has been at a Tvind Villa home for 16 years. He suffers from serious deterioration. His nickname comes from the fact that he was well educated, is intelligent and a feisty talker. He had been a soccer coach at schools. Since the villas are not at full capacity now, he has a whole building by himself. "I prefer living that way, alone. There is always togetherness if you want it, and that is fine. If I want that, I can always find it here," he tells me with a twinkle.

Tvind maintenance worker with special student helper hoping to use parts from this old tractor for another tractor.

Several school-boarding residences have their own ecological vegetable garden, small park and art works. While each residential group lives separately, most of them eat together especially at lunchtime. Everyone is permitted to deliver a short message at lunch time by tapping a glass.

Smoking areas are apart from the buildings. The main one is at the edge of the forest. Half of the 13 hectares is in pine trees they planted. Workshops, maintenance hall, and climate center with windmill museum contain the tools, equipment and vehicles necessary for near self-sufficiency. Tvind even has its own sewage purification plant.

Several buildings have posters or placards showing a common vision: "Alone the world changes you; together we change the world." "Don't talk about the change, be the change".

Tvind has several annual arrangements. Around 5000 outsiders participate at events and/or visit the grounds on their own.

Winter Concert, January 26. Involves professional classical musicians, dancers and singers from all over the word performing unique compositions on Tvind's international stage.
In winter sometimes many students take ski trips to Norway.

Earth Day, April 22, includes activities to protect mother earth.

Peace and Justice Conference, May 10-13.
https://www.counterpunch.org/2019/05/24/denmark-peace-justice-conference-based-on-activism-in-many-countries/

Summer Camp, July, for youth with limited means to get away for the summer.
Some summers there are theater performances by students and teachers.

DNS Boot Camp, July, this is 16 year-olds and up – an international event for another kind of education enthusiasts for a week of learning, connecting, action and cultural exchange. https://www.dns-tvind.dk/dns-boot-camp/

Hot Air Ballon National Competition August 7-10. Tvind's students have often won the national competition. They also travel to compete in other European national competitions.

"Tvind OL", September 13-14. Students from 30+schools and care homes where TG has a presence gather for two days to compete in 60 sport disciplines: table tennis, soccer, volleyball, archery, cycling, fishing, dancing, climbing, chess, darts, athletics…

Justas Story

"I got to know about PTG from my brother, who was a DNS student. He had seen a small add in a Lithuanian newspaper about Tvind's schools. He took the education and then taught DNS for five years before moving back to Lithuania.

"I wished to be part of a social environment, and learn some life skills. I was quite a lonely child, and quite well cared for living with my mum in Lithuania. I became good at sailing, even made a national team, but I was stuck at computer games too much, and too isolated.

"At the PTG boarding and day school for three years, I helped others in the more 'needy' category. I didn't have to pay, rather I had responsibilities in the school which covered my costs. I took care of the sports hall, tidied up Day School after classes, for example.

"I joined TG in 2013, because at that point my brother was in it. I was very impressed with the Teachers Group. Especially after having the privilege to travel the world: to Africa for a four-month bus trip. Also to Palestine, Sri Lanka, Russia. This center and college changed my life greatly. My worldview opened. I saw TG as a good way to grow as a person and be part of something that has a positive impact.

"After PTG, I started DNS in 2014 and graduated in 2017."

The Necessary Teacher Training College

DNS is structured in three annual periods. The mix is half time working while learning, and half study. Year one, Global reality": two months preparing for the four-month bus trip through western Africa. The aim is to get to know the people and to assist in projects underway. Then three months bringing what one learns to the European public. Then three months "saving up" for tuition by doing some pedagogical or other work.

Year two, European reality: six months with one's class moving into a flat in some European city to explore ordinary people and to get jobs. Students participate in the local community and organize cultural-political events. This is followed by three months of study back at school, and then three more months in Europe doing what is "most appropriate".

Year three, School reality: eight months of full time teaching practice in schools with care homes and or students with special needs. Student-workers are supervised by graduated teachers. One learns pedagogy, didactics and epistemology. Followed by four month study period back at DNS school. At the end, one takes the bachelor monograph exam.

A DNS slogan states: "2 teach is 2 touch lives – forever." Special for DNS (and DRH) *schooling*, as the TG calls their education, is the Doctrine of Modern Methods (DMM). It has three categories: *studies, courses, experiences*. DMM is a digitally based system. A computer is provided each student connected to the school's digital library containing 18 subjects each with scores of tasks.

One example of subjects is "Big Issues of our Time". It has 50 study tasks, some for the collective and some each student can pick for himself. Some anchor themes: "We need a future that is bright, green and free", "a new model of sustainable prosperity"; "We must decide which type of capitalism or no capitalism"; "defy and defeat capitalist globalization"; "doubt superpower politics and its constant wars"; "Lousy dictators must be substituted with non-violent revolution."

Those are not topics and points of view found in other forms of schools.

During the studies period, which is primarily individual, the student reads on one task for hours or days, not only what is in the digital library but also suggested books. He/she writes a synopsis and sends it to the teacher. There are usually two teachers for a team of from five to fifteen student-teachers. The teacher corrects the task and makes comments. Teachers act as assistants and advisers to students. Both live at the same facilities and are engaged in every aspect of the school, including cleaning and gardening. Daily pace is quick and constant. One is exhausted at the end of the day.

Study time takes up 50% of the program. Then there is the course period, which teachers or outside experts speak on a topic, and engages all in discussions. That takes up a quarter of the program. The remainder is experiences planned and performed by the team, and others by the individual.

The school is governed by the weekly common meeting. Anything related to schooling and living conditions, complaints included, are discussed and decided upon. Adjustments can be and are made.

Back to Justas

"There is so much individualism in the West; so much alienation. We must have a better purpose for living than our own careers and money. In Africa, I did investigations into agriculture and migration. We saw the poorest and richest, even hitchhiked with one very rich plantation owner. I learned that human societies are messed up, and this made me realize I needed to be part of making an impact. Africa, and the DNS schooling, gave me a broad understanding and a sense of belonging that nourishes activism.

"I didn't take this journey on my own. Other people help to guide me, to challenge me. Therefore, I believe travelling alone is not enough. To learn, we need people. Have you ever heard the saying '1+1 is more than 2'? Maybe it does not fit in math, but I believe this is true when we think of humans – we can do more when we stick together. We can complement each other's weaknesses. We can motivate and challenge one another. We need to meet the people on our planet, to work with them, to learn from them and to use our collective knowledge to make life better for all. That is my life goal, and I believe that we can achieve this through education – Another Kind of Education.

"This education has given me a lot of insight into the reality of people in the world, but also a strong feeling of injustice. I learned that there is a lot of inequality in the world, I found out that too few do something about it, and I decided that I want to be part of changing that. I wanted to be a teacher who fights for justice together with the people. A teacher who is not limited by the four walls of a classroom. The world is our classroom.

"What makes me feel attached to DNS is that students and teachers together shape the school, and create something bigger than ourselves. One quote that stayed with me throughout the DNS program is: *'You do not join DNS as it is, you join DNS as it is going to be.'*"

"My role in the school is the daily running, and recruiting students for the program. DNS is a unique model for future schools. I wish to spread the idea that it is possible to run another kind of school, and we are doing it here. It makes me happy to hear people getting inspired, learning about our way of learning, or if they choose, join us on this journey."

When Justas returned to Tvind from Africa, and then set out to bring Africa to the West, he participated in protesting coal mining in Germany. His six years of schooling at the College Community encompassed a lifelong education in itself.

Ron's Observations

Most of the students and teachers eat breakfasts held in smaller kitchens and dining rooms where their schools and boarding residences are. At DNS, breakfasts are always lively with talk, body movements, facial gestures, hugs, and maybe soft music.

Marian often comes by for a fruit breakfast. He was born in Romania but ended up in Germany for most of his youth before coming here to PTG at age 15. German social workers sent him to several of their special school but he was an uncontrollable rebel, so much so that one employee convinced the municipality to pay for his transportation and care at Tvind. Marion is now 30, a well-functioning paid maintenance worker living in a small rented house nearby, in Ulfborg.

At the common cafeteria, meals are simply marvelous. Something for every taste and particular diet: meat-eaters, vegies, gluten-free specimens. Many meals are prepared without meat, sometimes with fish, sometimes only vegetables and fruits. Annie Woods is the kitchen coordinator during her first year at Tvind's "saving up" period. While waiting to start school with DNS19, Annie plans the meals. This is a day's lunch and dinner menu: broccoli cream soup, eggplant bites, vegetable pie, baked potato, caramelized carrots, salad. Dinner with spinach lasagna, tomato-soya lasagna, beef lasagna, steamed vegetables & salad. Liquid is always water with lemon option, various milk products and juice.

Annie Woods initiated a FridayForFuture demonstration in the nearby town, Holsetebro. Around 50 Tvind students and teachers participated alongside a few locals. They were inspired by the Swedish teenager Greta and by their Peace and Justice Conference last May. Photo by Jenny Jagodics

It seems to me that the resident-students, in good health or otherwise, are well integrated. Most get along well with one another as far as I can tell, and there are arguments. Everyone in the regular school programs are constantly engaged. The overall DNS teacher council of seven educated teachers and two in training meet weekly, as do all the other schools' teachers' councils.

Piotr Dzialak is a young TGer from Poland. An avid reader, Piotr takes care of several administrative-coordinating matters and books. He tells me, "While we do concentrate on the collective rather than the individual, no one is left alone when in need, and all who need special attention for learning get it. We have long been accused of authoritarianism but the years I have been here, I see that we express what we wish including disagreements. Our process grows, transforms." – revolution must be permanent say sages.

CHAPTER TWO
Student Francesco

Francesco Maria Antonicelli (28) was born and raised in Bari, at the boot of southern Italy. Francesco dropped out of university just three exams away from earning a bachelor's degree in literature. He'd had enough of "surfing through life with my navel in the lead". Recklessly heavy into drugs and alcohol, he sought something bigger than himself.

We met at Tvind's International School Center (School Community) located in Western Denmark resting beside Madum Brook. This is his story, how he decided to "fight with the poor".

Francesco in front of a shelter built by boarding school youth at the Tvind school center beside Madum Brook.
Photo by Ron Ridenour

Francesco has been in this program three years. He has one year left to complete the education and exams to earn a bachelor monograph at the Necessary Teacher Training College (DNS).

"It's not that I rebelled against my parents. My father is a taxi driver, and my mother is a teacher and housewife, and were always supportive. In fact, my mother was proud when I protested the war against Iraq at the local NATO base and was removed by police. I was only 12 but I already knew that the capitalist system uses wars for profit and to rule the world. I flirted with anarchism, but it was mostly a lifestyle, which became self-indulging and unruly. I later joined the Communist Refoundation Party, a split from the original Communist Party. But there were always internal crises and splits. I lost patience."

Bari "Little Pearl Harbor"

That NATO base where Francesco demonstrated, the Gioia del Colle Airbase, was under fascist control during World War II. The British captured it in October 1943. The US air force also used the base. It was nearby at Bari harbor that an unintended, tragic coincidence occurred that caused Bari to become known as "Little Pearl Harbor".

Bari (population then 250,000) became the only European city to experience chemical warfare in the course of World War II. The public, however, was kept in the dark until 1971 when Glenn B. Infield exposed this in his book, "Disaster at Bari". Franklin D. Roosevelt, Winston Churchill, and General Dwight Eisenhower had ordered records of the only chemical mustard gas explosion destroyed. Some records kept hidden were declassified in 1959. Gerald Reminick wrote another book, "Nightmare in Bari: The World War II Liberty Ship Poison Gas Disaster and Cover-up."

This is taken from Reminick's book. "On December 2, 1943 about fifty ships lay waiting at Bari, Italy for their cargoes to be unloaded. Suddenly, the German Luftwaffe thundered down…the raid became the worst bombing of Allied shipping since Pearl Harbor two years earlier. In fact, this attack became known as Little Pearl Harbor. [27 cargo and transport ships were destroyed]. A U.S. Liberty ship [John Harvey] laden with a top secret cargo of [60 kilo tons of 2000] mustard gas bombs received a direct hit and exploded, killing the entire crew and spreading its deadly toxic cargo across the water and through the air of Bari. More than one thousand Allied servicemen and more than one thousand civilians were killed…[US government silence about having mustard gas, its lies and cover-up is the cause for mustard gas seeping] through the world's oceans today."

Francesco says we must take responsibility and fight

"We can't just rely on political parties to change the world for the better," Francesco tells me. "We must also take individual responsibility and act too. I was into music and theater and I met a wonderful Italian artist. He had taken the Traveling Folk High School 10-month course. I looked into that and decided to take the three-year Necessary Teacher Training College program instead."

DNS costs 1000 Euros ($1,125) to enroll plus 8000 Euros ($9000) each year of study. This includes everything: tuition, room and board, traveling costs, equipment, books. Most of them who join don't have all that money so time is allotted to work at places in DNS's network of partners like the special schools that need teacher assistants, boarding schools that need caretakers, UFF-Humana that needs workers to collect and sort used clothing, and other places. But the DNS and 24-month Traveling Folk High School (DRH) don't just offer these jobs to pay for the education, because working is part of education: teaching and learning from other students and workers.

For admission, one must come up with the enrollment fee. For the rest, the school assists with finding employment for students for a year before starting the program. Francesco took this opportunity at a municipality-sponsored school for youth with special needs. The care home/school pays the teachers, assistant teachers and caretakers. Workers who are also doing the Tvind or Lindersvold DNS or DRH schooling then save up most of their wages to pay the program costs.

"I could make the enrollment fee but I needed to work for tuition, traveling and living expenses. I also needed to learn English and, at least, some Danish. The school administration helped me find an assistant job at one of the special needs schools, at Hellebæk on the east coast. I was there from August 2016 for a year. Those of us in the 'saving up' period met once a month for three days at Tvind to keep in contact, and come gradually into that environment.

"It was a crucial year for me, a revelation, fruitful, and I think for the children. We got along and they helped me learn their language. My threshold of explosion broadened. Not just a job, a life.

"Part of the education for the school community, including if possible those with special needs, is to travel and see something they otherwise would not. In my case, I was able to take five students for nine days to a farm close to my family in Bari. This was a great challenge for everybody concerned. The kids got their hands dirty working with the animals and the garden, and the farmer's family, and my own, fell in love with them. There were complaints and some tears but we felt happy most of the time. I don't usually think of 'happiness' but I did because the kids were happy.

"My family and some of the kids still keep in touch. One of them now has his own musical band even though he still lives at the Hellebæk boarding school-home. Another one is studying at a regular school. They are all flourishing."

Madum Bæk and Vikings

Madum Brook babbles, winding over ocher-covered rocks around Tvind, through the fields of grain and into a lake with the same name. I wondered why the name "Madum", confusingly similar to madam, and why "Tvind" as well? The local historical archive worker did some research and came up with this bit of history.

From late eighth century to 1066 Scandinavian Norsemen (Germanic people) dominated north-central Europe. This was the Viking Age infamous for its brutal raiders with long boats and large sails. Viking warriors made the best swords with which they murdered, raped and plundered people throughout northern Europe, down to France and Italy, over to Ukraine and even Russia. In northern England they slaughtered monks, royalty and lay Christians. When not killing they traded with some people, and learned Old English. The word meadow became madum. When some Vikings settled in western Denmark, they gave that name to the brook ("bæk" in Danish) and lake in the meadow area where Tvind is now. The first recording of this is in a bishop letter from 1274. By then Denmark's royalty had become Christian, a religion the last Viking leadership adopted. So the parish in this area took on the name Madum for its church and district as well.

In the local Danish dialect of that time, Tvind had two meanings: twisting and binding – the brook twists, winds, and a rope is twined, weaved. The anti-capitalist teacher-warriors who settled at this place wished to bond and thus kept the term Tvind for their school cooperative/community. And when they built the world's largest windmill, it was named Tvindkraft (Tvind Power).

Traveling to Africa

After a year at Hellebæk, Francesco joined the DNS 2017, September 2017. "We were 14. We're down to nine now. We started studying Africa. Each DNS class either buys a used bus or takes over the previous class' used bus. We fix whatever is needed for the West African trip," Francesco explains. "A used bus is always decided upon not just because it is cheaper than a new one, but because it is part of the education, a survival part of learning to live with 'self', in a 'team', all within 'environments'. I trained for the driver's exam and became one of the chauffeurs.

"In our preparation period, we learn that while we won't understand everything we can focus on various environments and living conditions, and learn some skills useful to survive and to build bridges. I usually feel somewhat outside modernity. I'm more anachronistic, closer to ancient Greeks where the term comes from. But with this school community, I felt and feel less so. I even began writing again, stream of consciousness to help me understand today's world."

Francesco had known Guendalina well before coming to Tvind. She followed him and is part of the team as well. Guenda studied philosophy and graduated with a masters. (Her story comes next.)

"Guenda and I have talked a lot about philosophy – human beings past, present and what is in store for our future. Will there be redemption for our sins? Through this process, and especially here, I am much less self-centered, which is nearly a requirement in modern Western society in contrast to learning to live and connect with all humans.

"The African trip is conceived of as professional, political and personal. We realize that 'fighting *with* the poor' is not the same as 'fighting *for* the poor'. We reject the white-guilt paternalistic syndrome. A good pedagogue is not a 'savior' but a guide; not a leader but a mover." The 14,000 kilometer round trip by bus is challenging in many ways. There are always some repairs to be made, sometimes by the team, sometimes by paid mechanics. The bus becomes the team's bedroom and kitchen. They make toilet stops at facilities They also sleep in tents beside the roads.

The four-month trip is the travel-educational experience itself plus assisting in some projects, which TG supports in Senegal and Guinea Bissau. They also engage in investigations into local and national conditions and customs along the way.

Once crossing from Spain to Morocco the team learns something about the Sahrawi people in Western Sahara, which is still under the thumb of Morocco against UN laws. Mauritania had helped Morocco keep this people down but turned over their "territory" to Morocco, because the expense was too great. The Sahrawi Polisario national liberation front also cost their occupiers too many lives. Western Sahara had long been a colony of Spain.

The most dramatic part of the travel from Denmark to Guinea Bissau for Francesco was in Mauritania where he and two others formed an investigation team to learn about slavery.

Slavery in Mauritania started long before European colonialism and continues today. Although outlawed in 1981 by presidential decree, yet not criminalized until 2007. According to native abolitionists, not a handful of slave owners have been punished.

Descendants of black Africans, called "black Moors" and "Haratins", captured during historical slave raids serve lighter-skinned "white" Berbers or Berber-Arabs. Many of the latter are offspring of slave-owners through centuries. "Chattel slavery" of adults and children are full property of their "masters". Regardless of the new law, slaves can be bought and sold, rented out, and even given away as "gifts". Slavery exists not only in rural but also urban areas, and women are most affected. Women slaves are often kept for sex and live with the domestic animals. Some "masters" won't let them pray because once born into a caste they are unworthy of having a god-Allah.

Mauritania is nearly totally Islamic, Sunni Muslims. Abolitionists are often jailed – accused of being anti-Muslim or anti-Islam. Abolitionists and other critics of slavery assert that between 10% and 17% of Mauritanians are enslaved. Some place the numbers as low as 40,000 others as high 600,000 of a 4.3 million population.

http://www.stoppingslavery.org/slavery-in-mauritania.html

"Usually, local people open up to us, because they surmise that we are not tourists, not normal white travelers, because we don't dress up and we travel and live in an old bus," Francesco says. "When we saw kids praying by a road in southern Mauritania they showed fear in their eyes once we stopped to talk. Communication was mainly through gestures, but our teammate Louisa from Morocco speaks some Arabic. She got the impression that they had never seen white folks.

"A Western-dressed, light skinned black man came. He spoke English and French, and so could we. We asked him who these kids were and their names. He said: 'It is not necessary to know their names.' We thought he didn't know their names himself but he was clearly a 'master'.

"It turned out that he didn't live there but came for visits, because his family owned the land where the children were. He called them 'beasts', literally, beasts. At first, he was forthcoming with information. Without qualms, he told us that 'beasts' were not paid for working but received shelter and food. There was no official registration of their birth, which is one reason why there are no accurate figures of how many people are in castes, which 'qualifies' them to be used as slaves. Their status was determined hundreds of years ago. A few 'lucky' ones are considered worker castes, because they are used for a specific kind of task. The 'masters' don't let any vote.

"While he talked, the kids just watched, sheepishly. They were dirty and wore tattered rags. We saw the bourgeois man make a mobile phone call. Soon, a police car pulled up. The police told us we had to move on but not before we were to take selfie photos with their telephones. They said it was too dangerous to hang around here," Francesco ends this experience here.

"When we got to Guinea Bissau, the team I was in installed an irrigation system at a teacher training school run by ADPP Guiné Bissau. http://www.adpp-gb.org/programs/education/ We had learned how to do this from a farmer in Senegal. We bought the piping and a pump and made the system. Another DNS 17 team of three built a playground from recycled materials, much of it picked up from trash. The DNS class before us had built an oven there.

"During this time, most of us slept in the bus; others in one room provided for us."

"The Guinea-Bissauan DNS students and teachers are a lot like us in Denmark. Their lives are dedicated to this work – fighting with the poor – on a daily basis. Hardly any free time. Yet we could tell that they felt they are fulfilling something important for them and their countrymen. They don't have much material or money so the fact that we European DNS students come through for a few weeks at a time, year after year, with a few skills and a bit of money is definitely useful, and we are comrades at the same time," Francesco summarizes.

Upon returning to Denmark, Francesco and his two Italian compatriots brought their African experiences to people in Denmark, Lithuania and Italy. Two other DNS17 teams did the same elsewhere. Francesco's team came up with a unique method of communicating: "meet the others", showing photographs and drawings of people they had met in Western Africa, and then asking the audiences to choose who they would like to hear about.

People they had met on their journey had made most of those drawings about the word, "happiness". Tvind student-teachers took these to cultural centers, libraries, social centers, housing squatted by homeless, secondary schools, even an occupied former police stations which rebel-minded youths had taken over.

"This gave personal names to people who could have been caught up in the migration crisis, and some were," Francesco says. "One good example of why some people fled their land is that big corporations had forbidden them to fish their waters. The fish 'belonged' to the capitalists not the native peoples."

Francesco's team traveled those three months by hitch-hiking, riding trains and buses. In Italy, they stayed at his family's home. Elsewhere, they "coach surfed". Their expenses, which they had earned in "savings up" period, were minimal.

During the second "savings up" period, Francesco returned to the special school at Hellebæk, whose students were glad to see him again. He also worked in the local, popular café.

For the European Reality period they decided to live and find work in Malmo, Sweden. They rented a cheap three-bedroom flat with four beds in each. Francesco and his two Italian compatriots could easily find work in eating establishments. Others got part time or temporary jobs cleaning, assisting in pedagogic work, one got a painting job, and two couldn't find anything for three or four months.

"This was yet another real challenge. We were 12 people then from six countries," Francesco says. "With our common economy principle we put our wages in a pot for all our needs. Each gets a bit for pocket money. We had no problems with that. Bed intimacy was modest.

"Most of us worked part time and we all continued doing our study tasks, such as: life style sustainability, world history from the early civilizations east and west, contemporary Europe. Collectively we decided who does what chores and who prepares what for our cultural and political events. We reached out to the community we lived in, bringing to as many people as possible our African reality and what the School Community has to offer."

Francesco's long black hair and beard shake enthusiastically.

"We organized open house events, workshops and forums, and screened movies. We did some actions, too, like the 'dumpster dive action', in which we take food thrown out by markets whether they make it convenient to do so or not. We got most of what we ate this way.

"We participated in Friday for Future climate actions. At one rally, the Swede teenager Greta came and we spoke with this empowering girl.

"I think we created a positive network, one that might endure. We keep in contact with many we met in Malmo. Two of them came to the May 2019 Peace and Justice conference."

Back to Tvind for a three-month study period: social science, history, sustainability and natural science. At the time of this writing, each classmate is to decide what to do that is "most appropriate" for their education for three months – how to develop towards becoming a productive teacher and global citizen. There is a budget set aside from the wages they have collectively earned for this, enough so they can travel somewhere again either alone, in pairs of groups.

When they return to Tvind they will have eight months of teaching practice. Francesco thinks he will return to the special school at Hellebæk. Another possibility is taking a bus back to Africa to be an assistant teacher at one of their DNS colleges.

Francesco spoke of what he has learned so far: "Activity, experimenting, broadening my knowledge, and the common economy are the greatest lessons for me. I just love it. No matter what job I get at the end of my education here, I will always be a teacher somehow. Learning about the world and engaging others to make a healthy life for one and all is what life must be about. I still have to find my way of doing it but I know it will come."

CHAPTER THREE
Student Guenda

Guendalina Marzulli DNS17 student-teacher training.
Photo by Jenny Jagodics

Born into a working class Italian family inspired by art and music, Guendalina Marzull (30) never lacked human warmth. Her three year-older sister became an artist, while teenage Guenda thought of becoming a social worker after reading "One Child." This memoir by psychologist Torey Hayden concerns abused children.

Guenda comes from Bari where she met Francesco Maria Antonicelli when they were young students. Her parent are both post office workers. Her mother is from Sicily. There, daily life often is filled with Mafia horrors. Even as a child, Guenda supported those who challenged Mafia brutality. She thought of becoming a judge after they killed some judges. Nevertheless, it was philosophy that drew her most.

"We were all independent. We could do what we thought best, but we always cared for one another in my family. As such, I took up activism and philosophy quite early in life, hoping to connect, hoping to help others connect in a loving environment," she tells me gently.

"I am today who I am, in part, because I was fortunate to have great teachers. Philosophy felt natural to me. Reading these exciting outlooks opened my mind to think critically, experimentally. Though we humans often see ourselves as separate, we thrive best when connected.

"I followed my passion into activism and education. You can't be really good at something if you don't follow your love."

Guenda took her first philosophy class in high school, age 15, and continued into university. She felt such respect for this world of thought that she bought new books about philosophy instead of used ones.

Although Guenda leans towards anarchism, she is "realistic" enough to have supported the "common good" democratic socialist idea and its parliamentary center-left coalition. This 2012-3 electoral effort of the Democratic Party/Democratic Centre/Italian Socialist Party/and Left Ecological Freedom Party was distinct from mainstream politics in that it encouraged "social movement as legislators". These parties earned majority seats in the parliament but could not form a government.

Associated with this movement are the philosophical and political theoretical ideas of Ugo Mattei and Toni Negri, which have been introduced in several European cities at "Talk Real" seminars and you tube presentations.

Guenda was then juggling philosophy, occupying abandoned buildings, and conking out in a life style of drugs and alcohol.

"I was reflecting too much on human beings and not acting enough with humans. I was torn between wanting to go further with academia, becoming a professor of philosophy, or being myself. There were too many rules in academia," Guenda says frankly.

The seriousness of the study of philosophy, its universal language, its holism grabbed her intellect, also her feelings for humanity. But it was far afield from human struggle.

She received her masters of philosophy, in 2017, after five years of study.

"I felt dry. Not knowing where to go. A friend showed me an article about a traveling college education somewhere in Denmark. I looked up its announcements on Facebook. I took a chance and did a skype interview and then a three-day observation stay. I got hooked on Tvind and the Necessary Teacher Training schooling," she says.

To pay for the DNS college she worked half-a-year in one of Tvind's three Villas with disturbed adults, several with psychological-social disorders. Each adult is evaluated to ascertain what specific program would be best for him or her. This is called ITP (Individual Designed Project). It differs from the STU (Specially Designed Youth) programs for disturbed youth that offer some academic and life style educational courses. Tvind started this residential care program for adults in 2004. Municipalities began using it in 2006, and since 2014 the program comes under DNS.

Guenda confronted many challenges with these adults, at the same time learning Danish and English, and coping with Scandinavian winter.

"Persistence and authenticity, learning who I am deep down – these were qualities and introspections that matured me. This 'saving up' period is so useful. I felt ownership of my education. People only attending normal schools have no idea what they miss learning," she says.

"The African preparation time was exciting, fast and furious. My African experiences revolved around investigating who these people are, learning about them through their music and other arts. The Moroccan "*gnawa*" music reproduces the sounds of chained slaves, reflects upon the pain – a healing ritual.

"I met a Russian-Italian woman in Senegal who founded schools for children. She lives with the local people and is so tough – she inspired me greatly. Another woman from Gambia was still going strong at 81. It took her ten years to get the first theater built in Gambia, but she persisted and it is now a beautiful place for everyone, for people who never had such a space.

"Best is to fight with many for the common good. But if you can't find others to struggle with then one can find solo ways of making change on an individual basis. The point is to act!"

Guinea Bissau Liberation

Guenda looked into Guina Bissau (G.B.) history to learn why there is so much poverty, internal divisions and corruption. Why when liberation leaders led by the intellectual Amilcar Cabral and his half-brother Luis were progressive, and sought a socialist economy and egalitarian way of life?

Amilcar was an educated agricultural engineer, poet and theoretician influenced by Marxism. He associated with Angola's liberation leader Agostinho Neto, who led the Popular Movement for the Liberation of Angola (MPLA). Both men were close to Fidel Castro and Che Guevara. In fact, Amilcar Cabral is viewed as Africa's Che.

Amilcar, Luis and others formed the African Party for the Independence of Guinea Bissau and Cape Verde. They also engaged in guerrilla warfare like MPLA.

Just months before the "Carnation Revolution", in Portugal, Amilcar was assassinated in an internal feud encouraged by the colonialist government. His brother became the first president of an independent Guinea Bissau (1974-80). He too was assassinated, in 1980, in another internal strife. Among several antagonisms is racism imposed upon Africans by white Europeans. The Cabrals were lighter skinned black Africans than most others in G.B. Their mother was from Cape Verde, whose people Europeans treated less brutally and "integrated" them through sexual relations. These islands were uninhabited until Portuguese colonialists settled there in the mid-15th century.

White settlers created a population of mostly mixed European-Africans, as well as Arabs and Moors.

CIA analysts and many white politicians use the color-based variations to rationalize why Africans fight one another. Of course, economic advantages and disadvantages due to skin color nuances fostered upon the African peoples is not something that the white Establishment likes to admit.

"Guinea Bissau is full of contradictions. There is chronic fighting and stagnation – not something easily stopped. Most of their food is imported, and they are stuck in this monoculture economy. Yet I feel quite attracted to the people," Guenda says, her strong ivory teeth showing.

"There are less than two million people there; half-a-million in nearby Cape Verde. After liberation, they couldn't protect themselves against economic and political invasions by outsiders: white Europeans and North Americans, and some Africans as well. One domination ousted; another enters. It is the global market and its implications that take over."

Was there anything the people could have done better anyway?

"Yes, but it is not for me to answer that," the philosopher concludes.

Guenda didn't get much involved in the African DNS schooling, although she viewed it positively. She concentrated on investigations but did participate with a playground group. "It was a powerful experience to witness that we could make something attractive, fun and useful with so few materials, most of which came from trash," she says.

Guenda also felt secure realizing she needed so few comforts not only to survive but also to feel good. "My comfort zone is not delicate as my visits to the toilet areas can prove. I was often too excited to fall asleep when bedtime came. I learned another important tool, writing. I started writing at night to stop life, to rethink and harbor the good moments of the day."

Back to Europe

Guendalina's time reporting on Africa to Europeans and then experiencing "European Reality" along with the entire DNS17 class in Malmo encompassed more challenges that, when met and passed through, deepened the collective and the individual's sense of worthiness.

In Malmo, Guenda worked as a waitress. She often came home near midnight to a house full of roommates and local people whom they had met at their presentations (see Francesco's story). Guenda enjoyed their company, and to see that other Europeans were shedding their masks.

"We also talked bullshit sometimes," Guenda admitted.

She had always worked since age 17, earning money cleaning, picking grapes, waitressing. "But I was absorbed with life without seeing the meaning in it. Now I was integrated with other people, feeling proud of these times without being concentrated on my navel.

"I didn't have specific expectations of what I wanted to change in my life. I just did it! My daily life changed totally. I no longer suffer about meaningless things. I overcame that weakness of feeling lost, of having no perspective – a quiet ocean of nothingness," Guenda explains.

At this writing, Guenda's class started their last travel period, engaging in "appropriate time", thinking of the future.

"DNS promotes activism. This schooling helps one to think and act not primarily for yourself. Although the 'I' is engaged, it thinks of what can help the community. DNS teaches skills for your life, and that are useful for others. DNS does not violate the self, one's values. It simply shows that to best feed our bodies, our minds, and our hearts is to feed others as well. While it is good to follow one's instincts, one needs a bigger perspective.

"I would like to have in my future something like what DNS has done for me up to now. Not to be alone, to be working, fighting with others for a real future for everyone. I am really attached to my homeland, to my origins in Italy, but it is not enough in itself – this Latin passion, impulsive, spontaneous behavior. I look forward to learning where all this will lead me," Guendalina reflects.

CHAPTER FOUR
Practice Teacher Simona

Simona Navadonskytes, student teacher in practice with DNS17. Photo by Jenny Jagodics, DNS17 student.

Simona Navadonskytes, born in Lithuania, 1991, is working with DNS 17 class as part of her third year practice teacher training. The educated teacher is yet another Lithuanian (daughter of two Russians), Svetlana Kosenko. She was a student in the DNS13 class, and this is her first job as a teacher. She is in the Teachers Group (TG).

I wondered why there are so many Lithuanians at Tvind, also at the Traveling Folk High School (DRH) in the Danish sister school at Lindersvold. Lithuanians number one-third of the three dozen DNS and DRH students now. I met Jonas, also Lithuanian, at Lindersvold. He was making a video documentary of the DRH program. Jonas and his wife had taken DRH training on the Caribbean island-state of St. Vincent and the Grenadines.

These islands (pop. 120,000) gained their independence from Britain in 1979. This island-state joined the pro-socialistic Bolivarian Alliance for the Peoples of Our America (ALBA), in 2009. Started by Cuba and Venezuela, in 2004, today there are nine member states.

Jonas helped make a video documentary of the program there, and later was offered his current task. He told me why so many Lithuanians leave their Baltic homeland.

"We were part of the Russian Empire and then the Soviet Union for two centuries. Since we got our freedom (1990), we are having a difficult time finding our national identity again. Several people became criminals and formed a kind of oligarchy, just like many did in the new Russia; some of them members of the Communist Party, too.

"When we joined the Economic Union (2004), many of these criminals traveled around Europe preying on other peoples, unfortunately. Others, myself included, traveled throughout Europe and abroad seeking new experiences, new jobs, a new life. So, some have ended up with Tvind and Lindersvold, and sister schools."

Simona is part of the first "free generation", she tells me. Her family and friends sought to find a new way of living and looked westward. She studied psychology, and graduated college with a bachelors. Then she traveled to Canada before deciding what next.

"I wanted more education but not in the 'normal' setting. Searching internet, I stumbled onto DNS through facebook. I came to Tvind to check it out. I liked the community lifestyle. My background approximated Tvind in that we lived in an extended family in a small rural village. Here, I felt a 'calling', if you will."

She enrolled and went to work at a special school to earn her tuition for DNS16.

"My psychology training was a bit useful there but not much. The staff put me together with a teenage girl who had various disorders, including problems with eating and lack of self-worth. At first, I felt this was too much of a challenge. We counselors and assistants had to get police training to learn how to restrain her, because she would try to harm herself. We achieved some success, helping her to express herself through dancing. I realized how lucky I was to have caring parents.

"During that year, we were three DNS16 students 'saving up' at this school. I am in total agreement that it is best to work for education, as part of education, rather than having all the money upfront or loaning it. This method and this campus allows one to feel you are part of something bigger.

"During the African study period, we bought an old Danish bus (1986) for the four-month Western African trip. We only got as far as southern Spain before it broke down.

"The bus stopped at night on the highway not far from Malaga. We were towed to a mechanics garage. The owner was so sweet. He let us stay in his garage in the bus. We used his bathroom and we made our meals in the bus, usually, where we slept too. We worked with a mechanic to replace the engine. The replacement was an old ship engine. We got a big break in the expenses.

"We were 13 students and two teachers. We did a bit of studying during those ten days in Malaga. We investigated the educational system talking to people involved in it. Three of us were Spanish speakers so we got along.

"The yellow bus was our comfort zone. It was part of the pedagogy aspect of our three traveling conceptions – plus the personal and the political – *fighting with the poor*. When local people see 15 people traveling and living in what appears to be a school bus – and usually the Tvind buses are just that – their guard falls by the wayside. We experienced this as well in our time in Africa, because we had more breakdowns although not as serious as the loss of our engine.

"This form of traveling helped us be accepted, and allowed our investigations to bear fruit. We were not viewed as typical white middle class tourists. This enabled us to see who Africans really are and how little we know about their world. Western politicians and the media distort their reality, and manipulate us to consider them as 'backward' people. But their poverty or lack of skills is not anything biological, rather is caused by continued colonialization, albeit neo-colonialism without direct 'ownership' of their countries," Simona says quietly yet pointedly.

"Our investigations dealt with the problem of slavery in Mauritania, women's rights, food sustainability, why there is so much poverty in lands of plenty, why there is so much corruption, so much debt, and the civil servant mentality."

Simona emphasized that the major economic problem is the lack of manufacturing facilities and technology to process their natural resources: minerals, fossil fuels, natural fruits and edible plants.

"All our classes that spend time in Guinea Bissau, for example, do some work with the cashew nut fruit. Until very recently there was no manufacturing processing in the country of this all-important food source. The fruit is usually exported to Europe where processing occurs. There is some manufacturing in Guinea Bissau, but the plants are owned by foreigners, usually Portuguese. The Africans are made to do the hard work for nearly no wages, and thus are kept in poverty and without formal education for the majority, or just a few years in primary school."

Eighty-five percent of the two million population is dependent on the cashew nut. The country achieved independence in 1974, due to the "carnation revolution" led by progressive Portuguese military officers and civil resistance to the clerical fascist governments of half-a-century.

The Portuguese still use G.B. as a monoculture resource: the import of unprocessed cashew nuts. Like all colonialists, as well as most neo-colonialists (and even the former Soviet Union), third world countries were/are kept poor, in part, by denying them the technology to process their unstabnatural products. Unfortunately, national governments have been unstable since 1974, political corruption is rampant, and governments do not help their people build their own factories to process cashews. Another downside is that this monoculture destroys the natural forests of other types of trees and plants, just as occurs in tropical countries with palm oil.

The work of processing is hard labor and time consuming. Without a factory process, each nut must be taken from the fruit by hand, dried in the sun, then roasted, cooled down and then baked before it can be eaten. Some small farmer-families do this work in their backyards but there is little profit in it, and the nation as a whole does not benefit. What usually happens is that the nut is taken from the fruit by hand and simply shipped abroad for processing. One can eat the fruit or wine can be made, but foreigners don't partake in that.

https://www.youtube.com/watch?v=du1MN-LoQ-k

"Africa is the high light of the three-year program, without a doubt. It opens your eyes, gives one strength to go forward. It forces your mind to think critically, not to take things for granted, to see the big issues within a global perspective. It really does teach you to learn how to learn. You ask yourself: what does it mean to be a teacher? Beyond being a job, it is a mission, a whole life.

"For African DNS student-teachers, this education means that to them too, but they are also bringing basic knowledge to their youth in rural areas where they might otherwise not even learn to read and write. With the DNS perspective, some children also learn to become leaders with stamina, helping to lead their people out of poverty and Western neo-colonialism. Otherwise, normal school teaching is usually indoctrinating so that youth are made to accept their lot," Simona explains.

"When we returned to Tvind we did our 'bringing Africa to Europe' experience. In Lithuania I had 15 events at youth centers, day care center, primary and secondary schools, the university where I graduated, and a women's prison," Simona says.

"At the prison, the women heard something quite distinct from their own lives. We did a sensory journey: tasting African foods, hearing African music, wearing their clothing. The women really enjoyed this."

Simona then returned to Tvind and participated in the Peace and Justice Conference. She expects to work at the Hellebæk special school managing interns after graduation. It may be that Simona will return to Lithuanian with an idea in birth for a new school community.

"At Hellebæk social village, I experience trust, a fulfilling development. Students enjoy being at this beautiful location. We are four-five teachers and interns for 10-12 students," Simona concludes.

Me as "course expert" and study group observer

Since the study topic this week was on historical events in which students pick one or two areas to study and present, Cuba-US history became a choice for some. My expertize in this case was the fact that I had lived and worked in Cuba for eight years, and written six books about the country and the ongoing US attacks against it. My favorite teacher and mentor is Che Guevara. He didn't write much but his long letter-essay, "Socialism and Man in Cuba", entails a vision I cherish most. Here is my favorite passage: https://www.marxists.org/archive/guevara/1965/03/man-socialism.htm

"Society as a whole must be converted into a gigantic school...To build communism, you must build new men, as well as the new economic base...Let me say that the true revolutionary is guided by great feelings of love. It is impossible to think of a genuine revolutionary lacking this quality. Perhaps it is one of the great dramas of the leader that he must combine a passionate spirit with a cold intelligence and make painful decisions without contracting a muscle. Our vanguard revolutionaries must idealize this love of the people, the most sacred cause, and make it one and indivisible... One must have a great deal of humanity, and a strong sense of justice and truth in order not to fall into extreme dogmatism and cold scholasticism, or an isolation from the masses. We must strive every day so that this love of living humanity will be transformed into actual deeds, into acts that serve as examples, as a moving force."

This study period week also dealt with how to decide what to choose to study, and how to present it to the whole group and to the two teachers and "experts", such as myself.

Students discussed how history can be known, and how it is written – by the winners of wars and empire leaders thought most. Yet the losers have memories that often are passed on for generations. Anthropologists surmise that this hand-me-down history can last about 25 generations, or 500 years. Nevertheless, accuracy cannot be taken for granted, and usually the causes of events passed down are missing.

Important also is the role historians play. Can they be objective, or do they cater to employers or to a political ideology? What about our own historians, our own writers? Can we be trustworthy, or do we leftists also fall into the category of "true believers", who fudge on accuracy, on telling the whole truth as much as it can be known?

The bus accident

The next course I was to present was cancelled suddenly, because the Tvind school bus was hit by a car. Thirteen upcoming students in DNS19 class were riding in it. The bus landed in a ditch, and several youth were injured. There were no deaths but two had minor operations for fractures. Kitchen coordinator Annie's face was swollen blue and one eye closed, but she will recover. An elder couple were in the other car and had to be hospitalized for a time.

Headmaster Annica, who arrived at the scene quickly, later explained to fellow DNS students that the accident was due, in part, because of the rain and a harrowing curve. DNS19 students were on a day's tour to a special school north of Tvind when this happened.

It was heart-warming to hear how effective and caring the emergency and health personnel acted. Ambulances and firemen were alerted by drivers who saw the accident. They all arrived within a few minutes. The older pair could not get out of their car until metal was cut away. A helicopter came to take them to a hospital. Ambulances took several students to two other hospitals. Police were helpful and polite. A psychologist was summoned and in the coming hours spoke with all accident victims, one by one. He also advised Annica how to handle the students when they returned to the college campus. And when they did return later that day or the next, they were met with warmth without "interrogations".

This was the worst vehicle accident Tvind had experienced since its beginning. Despite this frightful event, all five youth who were visiting the school to assess whether they would join DNS19 or DNS20 or not, and who were on that bus, decided to take the schooling. They were from Germany, Hungary, Slovakia and, yes, two more from Lithuania.

CHAPTER FIVE
Day School Headmaster Birthe

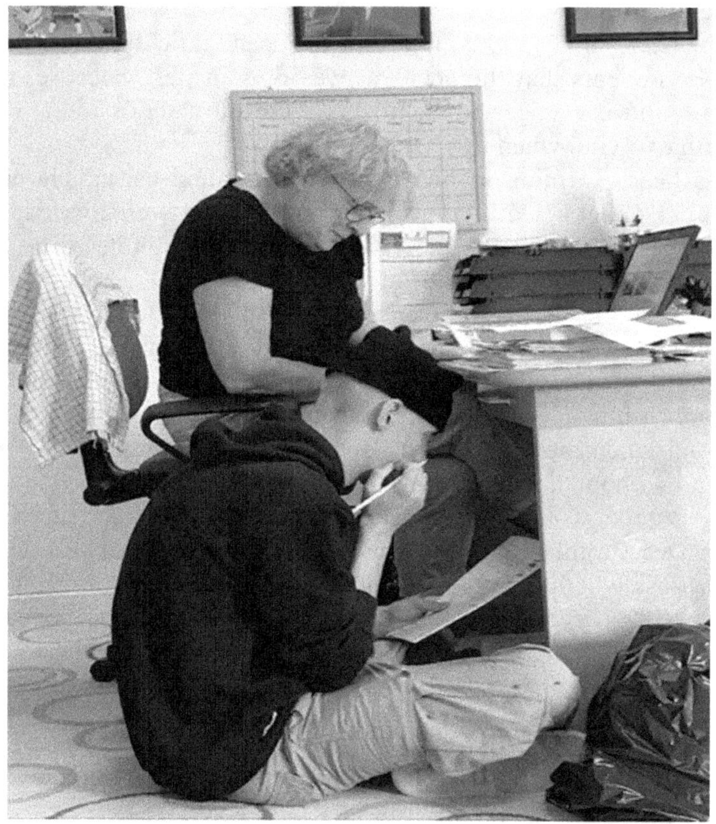

Birthe Norskov, day school headmaster, confers with
student, who pops into her office.

Birthe Norskov is an educated Danish teacher, the only Tvind-related teacher I interviewed who is not in the Teachers Group (TG), and the only one who lives on a farm.

"Our farm we live on counts 48 hectares. In addition, we have the 46-hectare farm that previously belonged to my parents. We don't grow anything now besides grass for the animals and the making of hay for the winter. We have 11 horses, five cattle, eight pairs of geese and 30 young ones that we slaughter for Christmas, an uncountable number of pigeons, likewise with hens and chickens. Finally, we have cats to make sure that we don't have mice or rats," Birthe tells me cheerfully.

"My husband is an agronomist and was my teacher when I went to agricultural school. The minute I saw him my horizon was in flames and I knew he was the one. It took some time to convince him (a couple of months) and we are still together after 36 years. We have no children, by choice. I don't like the idea of somebody else being dependent on me.

"I have made this dual life, one can call it, because I thrive with both of them. The farm is for me and my husband's needs and pleasures. The Day School is for my practical needs, too, and my desire to be useful for other people."

Birthe came forth in 1955, the first of two children born to a couple of farmers.

"I have always been loved and for that reason life has come easy to me. My childhood was without any obstacles and adversities. My brother was born in 1963, so I lived the life of a single child for quite some years. My parents have always been poor and that has taught me moderation and frugality, and I'm grateful for that – qualities that have made my life lighter in many ways," the energetic woman tells me.

"I enjoyed school and did well. I specialized in physics, math and chemistry, and finished in 1975. Then I travelled to New Zealand and found work there. A wonderful country and a wonderful place for me to mature. Well, once back in Denmark again, I started to train as a bio-analyst at the hospital in Viborg. After graduation, I worked at the hospital, and in following years I was also active in the trade union both as a member of the general board and as local president.

"In 1990, I decided that it was time to change careers. I enrolled at university in Aalborg and graduated with a degree in English and pedagogy, in 1994. I found a job teaching English at gymnasium in Viborg. Here I worked for five years until I started at *Småskolen Christianshede* (a Teachers Group-related school with troubled youngsters). In 2018, I was asked to take over the daily leadership of the day school here."

The only drawback with Birthe's farm life is that she is also glad for her work as headmaster at Tvind's Day School. This means that four days a week she drives 200 kilometers back and forth.

Tvind started the Day School in 2002. It receives most of its students from the local municipality. There are two categories: needy youth (18-24 or somewhat older), who are able to take a two-year post-secondary trade school program for the job market. They can take the final examination but it is not obligatory. The other category is for youth (some younger than 18), who may not be able to handle normal educational courses. Some of them have not learned simple survival skills, such as how babies are made. These youth are primarily taught life skills: how to express themselves so that it makes an impact on themselves and others. Additionally, they are encouraged to learn how to cook; how to keep themselves and their immediate environment clean; to take care of their health; learn elementary first aid; perhaps how to communicate with officialdom, which is becoming increasingly more difficult for most citizens.

The Day School also offers youths, who are capable of learning, what the Teachers Group believes is essential for all, what they call "solidarity humanism". The regular courses for the more capable include: Danish literature and other art forms; Danish and European history and politics; the English language; UK and US history and politics; world social studies; mathematics, geography, biology, chemistry, religions.

Topics could also include: music and poetry as a means of expressing political and social necessities, like: peace and equality, why there is poverty and how to eliminate it, what is the "American Dream" and why that ideology harms other peoples, what was the Cold War all about, and why another one will be catastrophic for humanity and the planet.

The Day School currently has 14 students in both categories.

"PTG and Day School cooperate closely, but they are two different units. Day school is an internal Tvind school, and every resident can participate in it," Birthe explains this somewhat complex structure, which aims to provide for each person's special needs.

"Both schools practice STU [*Særligt Tlrettelagt Ungdomsuddannelse* or Specially Designed Youth Education for each student], plus normal education courses, life style, traveling. PTG is the residence for both groups of youth. Madum Brook nature project is a program at the Day School. It is a practical programme focusing on environmental issues."

Some of the troubled youngsters have: ADHD (Attention Deficit Hyperactivity); OCD (Obsessive Compulsive Disorder); Asberger (Social Interaction Disorder); autism, drug dependencies, criminal backgrounds, and violent home life. Municipalities pay for these youths' boarding care and schooling at Tvind, and have the duty of inspection.

"Many kids who come have little self-esteem," Birthe says. "Some young persons cannot express themselves adequately or even look another in the eyes. We have helped many to trust us such that they can relax enough to raise their eyes and look into ours. It means something wonderful when the child can see adult eyes that do not mock him, that do not reject him. He is then not afraid to open his mouth and speak.

"Everyone can learn something if they are given a chance," Birthe says.

All students can take an annual three-week trip to another country, if they wish and are capable. Last time they travelled to Malaysia on a study tour they called "saving the planet". The students helped pick up plastic caught in mangroves. This experience led to a teacher-student unique remake of a famous Hans Christian Andersen fairy tale, "The Little Mermaid."

They were rehearsing when I was there. The original story (1837) is a journey of a young mermaid, who is willing to leave her life in the sea in order to gain a human soul. Day School's version: the mermaid wants to become human and seeks out the octopus (witch), who will help her kiss a boy. At the same time, her father and fish friends show her that plastic is overcoming their sea and they will die out because of that. The Little Mermaid meets her boy, but he is also against polluting the sea. They see fish entwined in plastic. The Little Mermaid is torn: give up her roots, marry a human; or return to the sea and clean up the trash with her family. Guess how it ends.

How does Birthe gauge success of the schooling at Tvind?

"Our main aim is to help each person learn to conduct their own lives. It is not possible for many. The least that can be achieved is that each young person acquires some knowledge, some skills that allows him/her to cope better than without this education and care.

"Some of our troubled youth have passed the trade high school examinations and obtained work. One has even become an engineer, another worked with others to rebuild a museum. The latter boy had inadequate parents, stupefied in drugs and alcohol, who did not take adequate care of him. He wrote us a letter: 'You people did not give up on me. You helped me believe in myself.'"

Common Ownership and Municipality Feedback

Practically every municipality sends "special", "needy" youth, and many adults needing special assistance to private care homes and schools, and many do so to Teachers Group-related schools. Most of the facilities at these schools are owned by *Faelleseje* (Common Ownership). It is a small business firm started by TG, in the 1970s, to comply with an increasing government demand that buildings where authorities send special students be owned by a private firm. Today *Faelleseje* owns around 50 buildings (schools and boarding homes), and five ships. It also owns some buildings in England. The municipalities pay rent to use their buildings. The price fluctuates according to "free market" illogic. Last year *Faelleseje* earned around $5 million for rents at 35 schools/boarding residences. To meet strict government requirements, *Faelleseje's* director and one other board member are not members of TG. Most of the other firm's six to seven board members are in TG. All schools and boarding homes are legally independent of one another, but there are obvious connections, and whatever they may be are legal. The key connection is a joint approach to schooling, and a belief that all people ought to struggle to end poverty and wars.

That said, government civil servants have been encouraged to be suspicious of what Tvind/Lindersvold/Teachers Group are all about, including if they are competent to care for these especially needy people. Teachers Group is watched more closely than all other private entities in this business, and some civil servants refuse to send their "clients" to these places. Therefore, not many social workers want to talk to media people about relationships between clients and Teachers Group schooling and care centers.

One who did speak with me is best protected by being anonymous, but, as is said in the media business, I know who this educational advisor is, who oversees "client" students and inspects the Day School.

"Many at my work disdain Tvind and Teachers Group," she begins. "I ask them what do they know to be wrong with what Tvind does with our clients? Although nothing is forthcoming, I am seen as being too close to that 'fuzzy' world.

"What I see is that these very socially challenged youths are improving their lives here. This small, integrated society strengthens them. The mix of 'normal' and 'abnormal', of people of many skin colors, nationalities and languages is healthy, and helps heal most wounded kids," she tells me.

"And the school and boarding care personnel are receptive to any critiques we come up with. Whenever we point out something that could be corrected, they listen and comply if it is not against their own professional values.

"I come here often and I see the youth thriving. It is a pleasure to come here. The food, the surrounding nature, the art works, the concerts – all this besides the classroom work and practical workshops – is healthy for them. They are more stimulated."

"You know what?" the social worker says, smiling, "A boy here recently took and passed the trade school education final exam with the highest marks. He is so much healthier today than when he came. His horizon is beyond himself.

"Some of the children and young people here have complaints. Most of it goes along the lines of not wanting to get up on time for classes. A few have left, but they are welcome to change their minds and return. I don't know of a better offer.

"Many want to continue here after the three-year assignment, but that is up to other people in the municipality hierarchy to decide, and there is always the question of our budgets, which the national government is constantly cutting back year after year," the social worker concludes.

Birthe speaks of her future

"I sometimes think of retirement, but I also want to hand over the Day School in good shape to the next leader. That means that we have to find that person before I retire. Anyway, I think that farm life would fill out my time easily once I decide to step down.

"I'm very attached to the farm where I was brought up. When my father died (nearly three years ago) and my mother moved to a flat in Viborg, I simply had to buy the farm, and paid my brother half its value. I couldn't live with the thought of some random person taking ownership of my fundamental background. That's one reason why I am not in TG. I like being an ambassador for Tvind and TG, but I have no wish to join. I treasure my own money, my own time and my own decision-making. I'm a social person but also personal in many aspects, and not interested in engaging in living in a collective," Birthe concludes.

CHAPTER SIX
Author Ron

Angry me protesting war and capitalism at the "Time for Peace" rally, in Copenhagen, summer 2015.

I was nearing the end of my time at Tvind when I met two dozen Tamils from India from the southern states of Tamil Nadu and Kerala, and one Tamil woman from Sri Lanka. Several of them had worked in India for the world's largest wind turbine builder, Vestas, and had immigrated to work at its headquarters in western Denmark. Tamil couples came with their children to see Tvind's windmill, which had bested Vestas turbines in the 1970s, and to hear Alan Lund Jensen, *Tvindkraft* (wind turbine) caretaker, tell the story.

What an irony that I should meet Tamils here, yet just more evidence that one cannot escape from this globalized world saturated with human-made tragedies.

In late May 2009, Amarantha, representing the Latin American Friendship Association in Tamil Nadu, wrote me out of the blue. I did not know her nor the Tamil people's struggles, but her group had read some of my writings about Cuba and the progressive ALBA alliance (Bolivarian Alliance for the Americas with 10 member states). She asked me to look into the Sinhalese governments' genocidal war against her people in Sri Lanka, which had just ended. Specifically, she hoped I would bring to Cuba and ALBA a protest against the role they had played, perhaps inadvertently, in politically supporting this genocide.

"It is a great shock for the people of Tamil Nadu to find that Cuba, Nicaragua and Bolivia, among other countries, have supported the Sri Lanka Government in annihilating the Tamil population in the Island nation…

"We here in Tamil Nadu celebrated the 80th birthday of Comrade Fidel by releasing eight books on Cuba's achievements in various fields" [over several years this solidarity group had translated 25 books about Cuba and ALBA countries into Tamil]…

"We are struck dumb and rendered disheartened and disillusioned by this act by those countries of Latin America on which we have pinned our hopes for the future."

I was most reluctant to act upon her request. I had recently returned from several months in Cuba, during which I had joined the 50th revolutionary anniversary celebration. While I had made criticisms of aspects of the government's economic direction and the lack of workers' power, Cuba was my favorite country and revolution. However, I could not in good conscience disregard this request from what was obviously a comrade organization deeply distressed by what appeared to be an immoral and opportunistic policy by comrade governments.

Merely conducting a minimal of research, I was appalled by what I was learning, even heartbroken by the immorality of leftist governments, many solidarity organizations and left political parties. After two years of research, article writings, verbal and written protests to Cuban, Nicaraguan and Bolivian officials, I wrote the book, "Tamil Nation in Sri Lanka". It was the most complicated and agonizing writing of my life. Just trying to understand what had happened and why between the two major peoples (Sinhalese and minority Tamils) since Sri Lankan independence from Britain, in 1948, was incredulous, absurd and insupportable. So why did Cuba/ALBA side with the bad guys? Here is the first paragraph of the first chapter of my book.

"I think that the governments of Cuba, Bolivia, and Nicaragua let down the entire Tamil population in the 'Democratic Socialist Republic' of Sri Lanka, and betrayed proletarian internationalism and the exploited by extending unconditional support to Sri Lanka's racist government. [They did so] on May 27, 2009 when signing a UN Human Rights Council resolution praising the government of Sri Lanka for 'the promotion and protection of human rights,' while condemning for terrorism only the Liberation Tigers for Tamil Eelam, which had fought the government in a civil war since 1983 until their defeat on May 19, 2009". *(See note at end of this chapter.)*

The answer as to why these socialist governments did this is much too complicated and historical to explain in this writing. In brief, they were motivated mainly by geo-political opportunism. To make this perennial schism between Sinhalese and Tamils all the more incomprehensible, all governments rightist and leftist either did nothing or supported the Sinhalese – mainly Buddhist – against the Tamils – mainly Hindu plus minority Christians and Muslims. Yet the conflict was not just religious, nor did economic outlooks matter much. The Yankees and Brit partners, naturally, always sent war weaponry and other material support to the Sinhalese, as did many European governments. The Zionists even sent their own pilots and war jets. Moreover, China also assisted the Sinhalese, and to a lesser extent Russia. In fact, in the last years of the civil war "Red" China backed the Sinhalese with more war and economic aid than any other government. China later received its dream commercial shipping harbor at the most strategic site in Sri Lanka, Hambanthota.

Speaking with Tamils at Tvind brought me back to their tragic reality. In 2011, I experienced Sri Lankan Tamil's agony first hand in Chennai where I met some during a solidarity-book tour. It hurt deeply hearing of the moral misery rendered these people by socialist governments.

Farming Sustainability

Quite a relief it was to spend that afternoon with my hands in the soil. Friday afternoons, DNS classes conduct "school management: main area cleaning, grass cutting, shopping, and gardening. We were 27 in all, including four teachers. Headmaster Annica Mårtensson brought her seven-year old son to the common garden. He clearly enjoys weeding and planting.

Most of the half-hectare of garden land was already sown. Now we sowed peas, onions and carrots in the remaining soil. Other schools have smaller gardens on the campus.

The common chicken area is cleaned this day as well. Twelve hens managed by two roosters lay just enough eggs for breakfast. Chickens here eat mostly kitchen leftovers. They don't have enough fresh greens but enough space so that they don't hack one another.

A local carpenter, Henning, has been hired part time to be the chief caretaker for the common garden. This "normal" 50 year-old family man has fallen "in love with these people," he tells me. At day's end, Henning hugs me.

I was sweating refreshingly, and decided to walk the nearby trail beside Madum Brook to the farmer neighbor. I found Gunnar Joergensen in an enormous barn where he milks his 300 cows. He takes a break from wheelbarrowing hay to talk with me.

"We've been here since my great granddaddy's time. He bought this land in 1896. My family is the fourth generation. This is home. I don't need to travel, although I was in the US for some months driving those gigantic combine harvesters. But that is not my style," he confides.

"We reorganized our farm in 1997 to meet organic requirements, and our daily milk yield rose by two liters to 35 liters."

Gunnar was happy to go into details about his farm and his Holstein cows after I told him I had lived and worked on an ecological collective farmland (Svanholm) in eastern Denmark for three years. I raised two flocks, one after another, of 2000 hens and some chickens for meat. Their area was near 100 Jersey milk cows, each requiring one hectare of land.

"We have 450 hectares for our Holsteins. They need more land than Jerseys, because they are much larger. We also have land for grain feed but still need to buy some," Gunnar says.

"We have a good relationship with Tvind folk. In the beginning, they were open. But once the government got after them they closed inward. We have never had any problems with them. In fact, we hire some of their students and borders to help out on the farm, and they pay us the going rate for leasing the garden plot.

"They take good care of their property, the land and buildings. They even sanitize their own wastes. In recent years, they have been reaching out to the surrounding community. I regret that I am too busy to attend most of their annual arrangements."

Sculpture Park from Zimbabwe

UFF-Humana (Development Aid People to People – see more about UFF in Maksim's story, number 14 in this series) support to Africa includes assisting with the sale and display of some of the world's finest stone sculptures made in Zimbabwe. The word Zimbabwe means "house of stone". Sculptures are made from spring stone and opal, among the best of serpentinite stones, containing magnesium and ferric minerals. They come in many colors and can be soft or very hard.

Volcanos 2.6 billion years ago cast up this remarkable bedrock in an area now known as The Great Dyke. Rocks here are unlike any others in the world, and are perfect for shaping sculptures. During four centuries in the middle ages, artists in the kingdom of Zimbabwe made sculptures and then suddenly stopped. Remains that have been found are bits of stone birds, perhaps the Chapungu eagle, which probably had spiritual meaning.

This mother stands at Tvind's Zimbabwe sculpture park.
Photo by Jette Salling

Five centuries were to pass before a few men began to make stone figures again, this time to symbolize their culture and their need to be liberated from the British Empire. In the 1970s, a white farmer helped start the Chapungu Sculpture Park, near Harare. In the 1950s, the first sculptors were unskilled men. A few women have since taken up what has become a professional art.

These stone figures of animals and people are known locally as Shona sculpture after the largest tribe engaged in this art. Since its rebirth, an art movement has begun to attract would-be artists from Mozambique, Malawi, and Zambia. Many skilled artists teach newcomers. Some works maintain the raw stone and some are polished. The best artists have been compared with classical Greek and Roman sculptors. Some Zimbabwe works stand beside those of Henry Moore and Rodin. Picasso and Braque were inspired by Shona art.

Tvind and Lindersvold are supporting these artists by buying their artworks. Tvind has a collection of over 100 of these sculptures distributed all over the campus.

Artists are paid one/third the sales price upfront and the rest when sold. HPP supports the Friends Forever, which the National Arts Council of Zimbabwe co-started. Since 2004, Friends Forever organizes hundreds of exhibitions, promoting sales in galleries and museums – from Barcelona to Boston, from Moscow to Boserup, Denmark.

Practical-Theoretical Basic Education High School

I was invited to share a grill meal with PTG High School students and personnel. One student's parents drove from Germany with juicy local sausages for the occasion. We were a score of people at the high school's long veranda under a seven-meter high roof designed by the Danish architect Jan Uzton. He is a friend of Tvind and the Teachers Group, and designed their associated Humana People to People Federation headquarters in Zimbabwe as well as Teacher Group's convention center in Las Pulgas, Mexico.

Before us is a large grassy area for ducks, chickens, two donkeys and a horse cared for by these students. It was twenty years ago that TG began this school. This Practical-Theoretical Basic Education is unique and so effective for many troubled youth that the regional government has been sending up to ten "needy" youth and 15 well-functioning ones (16-24 years old) on high school scholarships here ever since 2002 – and that, despite The Establishment's disdain for Tvind/Teachers Group. The boarding high school program is three years, but some youth can stay on if they wish and if regional social workers agree or have the ever-diminishing funds.

The boarding school is large: classrooms, office, 26 residential rooms, large living room with fireplace, TV and billiard table. They have a grand kitchen, and adjacent is a cinema. The whole school community is invited to watch a film of choice once a week.

All students are encouraged to become as self-sufficient as is possible. They individually and collectively plan weekend meals; organize the Tuesday café cozy time, which could be a karaoke gathering; wash clothes and bedding; see to it that everyone gets up on time; engage in gardening and other practical chores.

The educational program is tailored for each individual's needs and desires. They can take courses that regular high schools teach, such as mathematics and languages, as well as pick subjects outside that framework. The scholarship students take the regular high school curriculum, and graduate once passing examinations. Some special students take exams as well. Everyone who wishes takes annual study trips to either India or Africa, and a ski vacation in Norway.

PTG employs educated teachers and DNS student-teachers, and the scholarship youth also assist their special class mates. Students can choose their own teachers and adult advisors. Here, one learns to resolve conflicts together and without violence, using a dialectical approach to relationships and learning. The school attracts a diversity of people, mostly from Denmark but also from other countries. Many come precisely to broaden their horizons.

Paradise Madum Brook Nature Park

A new addition to the school community is Madum Brook Nature Park project.

Before Tvind was sanctioned by the state government in 1989 (more on that in next piece), Tvind had built a large swimming pool close to Madum Brook. Since there was no pool in the neighboring town of Ulfborg its residents were welcome. Years later, the town built its own, and Tvind's pool was abandoned. Instead, the beautiful forest and brook have been embraced for other common joys: a treehouse, an overnight shelter with bonfire, a bridge over the twisting rill, a kilometer-long dirt path, and an apple orchard.

Work began in 2013, and while the Day School-PTG paradise project is basically completed there is weekly upkeep and plans for growth. A recent construction is the mellow goldfish pond with spring water from Madum Brook, which people can see from the boarding schools and adult villas.

The treehouse is a favorite for all. Seven meters high, it is built on four sturdy tree columns. Its 5X5 meter-platform can hold an entire class. One climbs 25 steps up a metal-wooden ladder to the platform where a 3X4 meter-hut welcomes one and all.

On both sides of the narrow creek a panoply of foliage unfolds: yellow-white-pink-violet lupine, daisy, dandelion, poppy, anemone, and elder flowers – their delectable juice a cooling summer gift.

Beneath the majestic treehouse, anthills dot the soil. These busy creatures scurry about adding pinecones and needles to form mother earth mammary hills.

From this height, one sees and hears the brook trickling along. One tunes into black bird love songs, lecturing starlings, cawing rooks, and cheerfully chirping thrushes and nightingales. Frogs croaking from the brook lift eyelids closed gently to best hear our flying kin. Sometimes neighboring cow mooing accompanies the thrilling concert.

Anna Hoas was to drive south to Tvind sister school at Lindersvold quite close to where I live. At that time, she was commuting between these places on a weekly basis. Anna had taken on the task of being a guide, so I decided to tell her story. Teacher Group members are always busy doing their specific tasks so I took this opportunity to interview her as she drove me home.

Madum Brook treehouse built primarily by Day School and PTG students with other Tvind hands, 2013-16.

#

Note. See my Tamil writings on my website (http://www.ronridenour.com, between 2009-14), and my book "Tamil Nation in Sri Lanka" (New Century Book House, Chennai, India, 2011). It is relevant to know that before young Tamil rebels took up arms, Tamils had resisted genocide only by using Gandhi's non-violence methods for three decades, but to no avail.

I have had 13 books published, among them are: "Yankee Sandinistas: Interviews with North Americans Living & Working in the New Nicaragua" (Curbstone Press, Connecticut, 1986). I worked in liberated Nicaragua for many months, and a bit in liberated Bolivia. I was a press relations worker for President Evo Morales at the climate summit conference in Copenhagen (COP 15), in 2009. I have written six books about Cuba ("Backfire: The CIA's Biggest Burn"), and one about liberated Venezuela, "Songs of Venezuela".

My current book, and my most important, is "The Russian Peace Threat: Pentagon on Alert"
http://www.puntopress.com/r-ridenour/
http://ronridenour.com/about.htm

Anna Hoas and her canine companion, Daim, at Lindersvold school community. She promotes their path with the T-shirt, "Another Kind of Teacher". Photo by Jette Salling

"Thanks to the businessman's Rotary Club, I joined the anti-capitalist Teachers Group," Anna Hoas tells me during our car trip from Tvind to Lindersvold. She works with communications at Tvind's sister community. I was finished at Tvind and would be spending a few days investigating Lindersvold's Traveling Teacher's High School (DRH).

Anna is from Sweden anno 1961. Her comfortable, secure childhood mirrors that of white Western members of the Teacher's Group (TG). Most of them did not join this radical group because of the "generation gap" theory, rather deciding as a moral choice to "fight *with* the poor". The Establishment "humanitarian" entrepreneurs counter such morality with "charity *for* the poor."

Anna was born and raised on Sweden's largest island, Gotland. This Baltic Sea island-province has long maintained a stable population of around 55-60,000 people (Sweden: 10 million) – farmers and fishers. Its 8000-year populated history includes the Viking period, clearly in evidence by rune stones with pictorial motifs, a fortress, and 65 kilos of silver treasures found recently – the largest Viking treasures ever found – that these Vikings had traded and plundered for.

Anna's father was a popular criminal detective; her mother a teacher, who practiced collective pedagogy. Her parents saw to it that Anna enjoyed a well-rounded education, which included learning about and appreciating nature's beauty and its useful gifts.

In her teens, Anna learned that not all people in the world benefit from the social-economic gains Scandinavian workers had extracted from the owner class, fearful that the producing class would take the path of the Russian Revolution.

Although she felt protected, and had no personal need to fight for a "better life", Anna used her privileged background to stand with those not privileged. Through pen pal letter writing, she heard about people being murdered, tortured and imprisoned by brutal dictatorships, such as Chile's Agosto Pinochet. This led her to write letters to political prisoners through Amnesty International. She stood with literature and AI money collection containers in front of liquor stores on the island.

"I saw photographs of six journalists Franco had garroted. One woman looked like me. I also learned how South African activist Steve Biko was beaten to death in an apartheid jail cell. I saw and heard Sally Mugabe [wife of Zimbabwe's liberation president from UK] present Zimbabwe's liberation struggle at my high school when I was 17 – indelible images," Anna says.

"About that time, the Rotary Club sponsored me in a student exchange trip to Australia. Here I learned how authoritarian white privileged males can be. While I was used to hitch-hiking in Sweden and experiencing an independent lifestyle, Australian women were not allowed to do that, nor could they partake in pub drinking-lifestyle."

Upon returning to Sweden, Anna was ready for learning a new way of life. Coincidentally, she saw a poster for the Tvind Traveling Folk High School and that led her to enroll in a sister school in Halden, Norway (now at

Hornsjoe and known as the One World Institute). It started in September 1978, and received state accreditation and funding until 1983 when the state regretted and ended funding. No wonder! Teacher Group-led school outlook is that of the Greek polyhistor ideal: acquiring knowledge in many fields, embracing a holistic view of the world.
https://www.oneworldinstitute.eu/

The Norway school has had traveling education programs from 10 months to two and even three years. (See upcoming stories about similar schooling at Lindersvold, Denmark).

Anna took the traveling training program in 1980-1. Her study group flew to Peru and hitchhiked to Brazil during the military junta period (1964-89), which the US had assisted overthrowing a democratic government and supported harsh military rule. Her group also toured a bit of Cuba.

"One of the things that impressed me about Cubans was the genuine curiosity and internationalism of young people. When some schoolchildren heard that I came from Sweden, perhaps they were 12 - 13 years or so, they immediately launched into a discussion about Olof Palme. The former Swedish Prime Minister was now working for the United Nations on the issue of disarmament. What did I think about that? I hadn't really heard about it, but they were happy to share what they knew," Anna recalls.

Then they flew to Merida and hitchhiked all the way from the Yucatan to Laredo Texas, 2,500 kilometers. "Mexico was simply a transit country to get to the US. So, we broke up into small groups of two or three and hitched rides with truckers who were very friendly and talkative. It was quite easy," Anna says.

However entering into the "greatest country in the world, the United States of America" was a different matter altogether.

"It was too creepy to hitch-hike in the south with guys driving pick-ups with shotguns hanging in the rear window and confederate flags as bumper stickers. My group purchased an old Chevrolet, which lasted to New York. We gave it to some guy we met on the street."

What Anna and the other youths saw in the US shocked them. By that time, the war against Vietnam-Laos-Cambodia had ended and Ronald Reagan reigned.

"The love of the military, of their wars we witnessed was simply appalling," Anna tells me. "We couldn't find any peace movement. We did meet some black Vietnam veterans in Washington DC who criticized that war. There had been great protests. But war, in general, was still accepted. And we just couldn't fathom the depth of racism and inequality throughout the country. Twenty years later I was with another student-study tour as a teacher, and we visited the infamous Mississippi Parchment Prison as part of our study into the death penalty and political prisoners."

The Parchment Farm, as it is called, opened over a century ago as a work prison only for blacks, who earned the state money suffering under slave labor. In 1961, the prison was used to punish Freedom Riders, black and white youth protesting discrimination on buses. At one time, the prison held 300 of these resisters to racism, and forced them into chain gangs.

"The conditions we saw were sub-human," Anna continues. "Yet the guards were proud to show us around. They had no humility about murdering people there. They even invited us to see their gas chamber and said we were welcome to go inside if we wanted – yuck!"

When young Anna returned to the school in Norway, she was so energized by the determination the teachers possessed in the Teachers Group that she joined. At that time, 1982, she was 20 years old and raring to fight against wars, racism, poverty. Her first class took a study tour to Zimbabwe.

"I have been told that in the early days at the Tvind campus, it was hard times for the left in that there were so many eager people with conflicting ideas, especially about strategy and tactics," Anna says. "Some of the participants at the courses wanted TG to write up an ideological doctrine, even to form a political party, and many meetings were simply verbal marathons. Some people were disappointed that TG was more interested in just implementing a communal lifestyle instead of talking about theory.

"No doubt that Amdi [Mogens Amdi Petersen] was a key figure then. He did have knowledge about lots of things, a lot of good ideas that he was passionate about. Of course, he would stand his ground in discussions. There were others with quite extreme notions, such as throwing furniture out because such possessions were 'bourgeois', but we grew out of those extremes," she says.

Unknown to Anna and the whole school community, the political police (PET-Danish Security and Intelligence Service) had been tapping TG members telephones between 1979-81, attempting to connect someone with "terrorism".

Anna met some Danish TG teachers who had just started special schools for especially difficult and/or abused young people. Anna joined the "cool" teachers' small schools program.

These new schools for youths (13-18 years old) with troubled backgrounds began attracting many of them. Due to the unique education, many of them improved their lives. Sailing the Atlantic on a schooner, or riding in mini-buses across many countries, troubled Scandinavian youths were learning about new people and cultures, and learning to take responsibility. They also studied academic subjects, and partook in drama productions, even Dario Fo and Bertolt Brecht plays, and learned to fly hot air balloons.

Anna said that effectiveness evaluations made determined that if such youth stayed in this program for more than two years, improvement rate increased by 72%. That meant they were more stable, less abusive to self and others, not overdoing alcohol or drugs, and through with the tough guy milieu.

Government Seeks to End Tvind

By then, DNS (The Necessary Teacher Training College), developed at Tvind in 1972, was under attack. In 1989, Bertel Haarder, the Education Minister in the Conservative Party-led government, had decided to close some of the smaller, mostly progressive free schools. The one he most wanted to erase was DNS. He cut state funding for DNS schooling. TG had to invent a new mode of funding the education as a private and independent college. So, the state did not achieve closing down DNS.

On March 21, 2018, *"Altinget"*, parliament's newsletter, reported that Haarder admitted: "Yes, I have been instrumental in restricting certain freedoms," referring among others to his decision to stop funding DNS education. "Freedom presupposes a certain goal of common values."
https://www.altinget.dk/artikel/bertel-haarder-ja-jeg-har-vaeret-med-til-at-indskraenke-visse-friheder

Haarder, Denmark's longest seating minister, added that he did not regret restricting "certain freedoms that I have previously praised", including equal rights for all religions and cultures – Muslims – and even political viewpoints, first and foremost Teachers Group. In the same breathe he acknowledged the necessity of forbidding Nazis, Communists and Islamists the right to establish schools with tax funds.

Haarder thereby placed enthusiastic and dedicated teachers seeking an end to poverty in the same moral and political category alongside Nazis – responsible for World War II and the murder of around 80 million people – and Danish Communists as well. The Communists had led the fight in Denmark against these Nazis. These three quite disparate groups was Haarder's "Holy Trinity".

Haarder also announced that his "Liberal" party was not really "liberal", but rather a "party of people sharing common values". Only creatures born white skinned, and who hold "common values", are granted rights that all others are forbidden. Haarder had his "Good Danes" – adherents of Martin Luther feminist-burning Christianity and capitalism.

Incidentally – as if this matter is only an "incident" – when Haarder discriminated against Tvind schools, the Conservative government had just called for an early election, because it refused to abide by the majority decision made decades ago that Denmark would not allow any country to carry nuclear weapons on/over/in its territory. The rule was that captains of war aircraft and ships capable of carrying atomic weapons must be advised in writing that they cannot bring them to Denmark. When the Social Democratic party demanded that the Conservative government deliver such a letter to the captain of a US war ship known to carry such weapons, and which had docked at Copenhagen's harbor, the government refused to abide by majority rule. It called for an early election, yet won anyway.

The "Liberals" then cut out some of the "Tvind schools" (DNS) but not all school programs, which included anti-capitalist information. Not good enough roared the next government, the alleged "Social Democrats". They decided to smash the anti-capitalist schooling institution entirely – all except the special small schools for youth and adults suffering various disorders.

In 1995-6, parliament investigated schools belonging to the "School Cooperation Tvind" three times and in three reports found nothing criminal.

Social Democrat-led government appointed a "social liberal" party leader, Ole Vie Jensen, education minister. Jensen's party (RV) had many teacher members and voters, who felt that the Teachers Group pedagogy was catching on with too many young people – a threat to their professional lives. Some speculated that this revolutionary education could even threaten the existence of capitalism through peaceful means. Something drastic had to take place.

Special Anti-Tvind Law

Ole Vie Jensen introduced Law nr. 506, the special "Tvind law", on June 12, 1996. The two socialist parties in parliament opposed it, as did most lawyers and a few bourgeois politicians on the basis that it was unconstitutional to make a separate law only for one educational organization. One of the stipulations in the bill was that the affected schools could not appeal in the courts.

After Jensen assured the parliament that his proposal met constitutional requirements, the bill passed with 89 for 20 against, two abstentions, while 68 members disdained to even attend the parliament. The rationale for the law was that 32 schools affected were not "independent". This meant 1,580 Danish students and 300 foreign students were left in the cold, and the school community lost $20 million in state finances. All of the "after-schools" and trade schools closed down, but the steadfast TG would not let the state close their DRH schools permanently.

The mass media backed the capitalist lawmakers. The daily known for being "liberal" (liberal as in New York Times, Washington Post) ran an editorial comparing "Tvind schools" with Al Capone.

Some of the affected schools brought a court action despite the prohibition, but it was rejected. However, the Supreme Court accepted the challenge. In their deliberations, all 11 judges agreed, and some angrily, that the parliament had violated the 1848 constitution, which is based on the principle that all are equal before the law, and that the parliament cannot decide what is constitutionally legal – that is what the courts are for.

This is the only time in history that the Supreme Court turned down a parliament law. Nevertheless, the politicians were generally unimpressed. They refused to refund the schools they shut down or extend subsidies to the new ones begun on a private basis.

With the Supreme Court victory, several schools petitioned to get the government subsidy back. Parliament refused, and the courts denied their case, because some rules had been changed for all "free schools", and the high court demanded extravagant court costs just to present their case.

When parliament made its special anti-Tvind law, many TG members were dismayed with the arduous consequences. Half the 200 members of Teachers Group left Denmark to start somewhere else, and a few simply left the community. About 100 stayed in Denmark and started from scratch to establish a new set of institutions based on funding from local authorities or, in the case of continuing the DRH schools, private financing mainly by students they could recruit. Most of the DRH students then came from outside Scandinavia.

Court Case Against Tvind and Amdi Petersen

Teachers Group had not capitulated. Time to take greater measures to annihilate them.

"It really is like Jim Jones and Jonestown, where everybody is in the same reality and everybody is in a parallel world, and they have sworn an oath to create a better world," said Danish attorney Poul Gade, who prior to entering private practice was the chief prosecutor in the charities fraud case against Petersen.
https://www.revealnews.org/article/us-taxpayers-are-financing-alleged-cult-through-african-aid-charities/

Amdi Petersen had to be imprisoned because he was like Jim Jones, and Al Capone? Yet not even the Establishment contended Amdi had killed anyone, let alone poisoning 918 people, of whom 909 died. Amdi hadn't even lived in Denmark for many years when he was incarcerated in Los Angeles for seven months during an extradition trial. Before that trial ended, Amdi agreed to return to Denmark to face charges of embezzlement, fraud, and tax evasion.

Police had raided Tvind and other schools where TG members worked, and confiscated 81 computers. The state attorney general's staff spent nearly $2 million on accountant fees to find evidence of criminality, and found nothing. Then they spent $12 million on the court case over three years with 170 days in court.

On August 31, 2006, the court found seven of the eight charged innocent of all charges. The one found guilty had already confessed to minor charges of transferring funds from one account to another relating to collective property and not individual profiteering.

Innocent were: Mogens Amdi Petersen, Kirsten Larsen, Poul Joergensen, Ruth Sejeroee, Marlene Gunst, Christie Pipps and Bodil Ross Soerensen. Steen Byrner, who had been responsible for the daily economy, was sentenced to one year suspended imprisonment and two years probation. All but Poul Joergensen then returned to other countries where they had been living.

The government was so angry that it had so little evidence and lost the case, it appealed to a higher court, which granted its petition. So, they retried the only previous defendant who was still in Denmark, and found Joergensen guilty of transferring funds from humanitarian projects to TG-related purposes, but again without personal benefit. He was sentenced to two-and-one-half years in prison for that and for tax evasion. Four years went by before a new government decided to send out an arrest order for Amdi and the others for a retrial.

Merethe Stagetorn was one of the lawyers in the first court case against the eight. She comes from an Establishment family, and is nationally known for her judicial expertize and sense of justice.

She told the Establishment media, "I really think well of Amdi, his thinking and that of the others at Tvind. Their schooling started with new thinking, and some of that is now in public schools." ("Berlinske Tidende", December 31, 2015)

Stagetorn said that some TG members have left the community, and complained about aspects of it and some leaders, such as Amdi. But, she added, "Like in any family that splits up there are always some who are bitter."

"These teachers are all so painstakingly careful and thoughtful, and Amdi is a worldly man. That court case was the case of my life. It was extremely challenging and will go down in Denmark's history," she said.

In 2010, Stagetorn really broke with Establishment manners when she took the post of director of *"Fælleseje",* the firm that owns buildings, ships and other properties where TG work at various schools. In a 2014 biography of her life, Stagetorn explained why she took on that task:

"I wanted to show that the Teachers Group had done nothing wrong...I respect them for their integrity, their intimacy and their interest in other peoples...They also have enormous knowledge about literature and lead a very active cultural life. I met them also as people who burn so honestly with a goal of changing the world by helping people in need, and I never felt they had a hidden agenda or told polished truths, such as we lawyers otherwise experience."

She added that she had been with many TG teachers over a four-year period and did not witness any "luxurious living" as the Establishment likes to claim, as if the powers-that-be do not live such lives. Nor did she ever see any of them drink spirits or take drugs.

"I don't know why the Danish system isn't strong enough to accept Amdi as part of its diversity…I do see that they are too closed an enterprise, and there is a lack of accessibility. I asked Amdi about that and he said that they had tried to be open, to reach out for a long time but met too little sympathetic response. Well, I sympathize."

A police director, Jens Kaasgaard told a journalist for a regional newspaper, Jesper Markussen:

"That was the biggest single case I was involved in and it filled a lot in those years. But then [the Justice ministry] appealed and I haven't been involved since…We thought then that we were saving the world, which [Tvind/Amdi] had placed in danger. In reality, we policemen were being used in a game." ("Holstebro Folkeblad", January 9, 2014).

The whole purpose of the character assassination against this one man is what we can see in many parts of the world. Make an effective leader into a cult figure, a villain that the majority can be propagandized to hate, thus hiding what that person actually stands for, which is what the powers are dead set against. We see, for example, how the Western powers vilify President Vladimir Putin to hide the reality that he stands for world peace and sovereignty for his people.

Steen Conradsen told the Holstebro newspaper reporter that Mogens Amdi Petersen "is part of the fellowship, but the image that he sits on the other side of the earth and rules everything with an iron hand just doesn't hold. No one can rule free people that way."

This regional newspaper actually published a balanced and long article about "Tvind" that day (January 9, 2014), because it was Amdi's 75th birthday. Conradsen, a veteran TGer for 43 years, was allowed to explain his view. What upsets the Establishment about Amdi/Tvind/Teachers Group, he said, is that 3000 people (anno 2019) wanted to live collectively, sharing their economy, skills, knowledge and intelligence with one another in a long struggle to end poverty and wars.

"Nobody wants to write about our pedagogy, about all that work we do for the weakest of youth, or the enormous tree planting project in Africa we are engaged in right now. You only come when a scandal can be concocted or when you can bring in the Amdi trump card."

Back to Anna

"After the anti-Tvind law, we saw there was a need for juvenile delinquents who otherwise were often put in jails, because the state had no special schooling for them. This was a forerunner to PTG" [Practical-Theoretical Basic Education]," Anna explains.

Anna began teaching at the PTG school the same time that Denmark's Establishment asked its global protector to arrest Amdi in Los Angeles. Anna remained at PTG until 2016. She was with the Madum Brook Nature Project, which used fallen trees for building blocks.

Anna recounts how much the PTG student-borders love the OL Tvind games and the hot air ballooning. As I write, "Hot Air Balloon Team Tvind" just came in second out of 12 teams in the annual Denmark contest. Last year, "Tvind" team won the Danish championships. Aside from the competitive spirit, the hundred or more participants have a ball at this inviting campus.

"It is at our common meetings where we decide what to do, what and how projects can be created. The same as with the Madum Brook nature project in which students are intricately involved. Our process is not nearly like that in the normal, bureaucratically run schools. Our students are glad that there are adults willing to listen to them, and then to act," Anna says.

PTG and Day School built this shelter by Madum Brook where everyone is welcome.

I've been interviewing Anna off and on for some days. Right now, we are sitting in a café at a gas station having just filled the tank. Her phone rings. She speaks in English with a former student.

"You know, some of our graduated kids, who had been involved in gangs, are pressed to return. Several of them keep in touch with us. This guy wants to leave the country to get away from that milieu. So, we can advise them about school programs we know about somewhere in the world. That's what this phone call was about," Anna tells me.

Anna speaks about how many of her students have had the opportunity to travel and do something good while at her school. Students are active in the process of choosing a destination for their study trips, so when the "refugee crisis" hit Europe in earnest, in 2015, a group of students that had initially planned to go to India changed their plans.

"At a common meeting we quickly concluded that it was a no-brainer to take the trip to India, and instead we chose to make ourselves useful at one of the Greek islands."

So, the group spent time as volunteers at the island of Chios, assisting a local solidarity organizations, which gave support to newly arrived refugees in the form of food, clothing and activities for the children.

While I am drinking my first beer in eight days, and Anna a juice, her phone rings again. An African young man, who was at PTG, wants to enter another travelling high school trip to Africa. Anna gives him some pointers.

"I get calls quite often. Many former students keep in touch with one another. That is what is important to me – working with people in the cold, on the margin. If you are privileged you have a moral obligation to share what you know or have access to with those who need those resources. It is not their fault that the system promotes inequality and poverty.

"We must introduce our own privileged people to others' real world so they can see, so they can feel how unfair it is, so that, hopefully, they will do something about that."

Having spent more than 30 years working with marginalized youth – implementing inclusive pedagogy in an attempt to empower them to pursue their quest for a good life – Anna decided to call it quits.

"I felt that I spent most of my time contesting immoral and often unlawful decisions taken by local authorities about cutting funding for these youngsters in need of our support. We were making good progress but in many cases the needs of the young person were disregarded in favor of 'saving' money. This was very upsetting for me, so in the end I decided to quit."

Anna took a year to reconsider her options. When she returned to work, she took on communications and recruitment. Anna decided to use her proficiency in the IT world to setting up websites and advertising on the social media. This work had its tensions, too, but she wasn't responsible directly for others' specific needs.

How does Anna Hoas feel about TG life, now after 37 years in this collective?

"Teachers Group world is secure, in all ways. Here there are no outcasts. We all are allowed to make mistakes, and there are always people to pick you up. It is a great comfort to be in an environment where learning is always present, learning about new people, new cultures, new languages, new solutions.

"Had I not lived here I would have missed so much wealth of knowledge, of life. If one of us in our work does not make a success of some project, well, there is someone else to step in. Each of us does not have to have 100% success for the collective to have success. There is always a fallback.

"In that way, we are not susceptible to the anxiety that the individual worker has if she loses a job, a business venture, or a marriage. We build greater resistance. We keep popping up, going onward. Makes one feel brave."

CHAPTER EIGHT
Veteran Teacher Gert

Gert Tjoelker Traveling High School Teacher at Lindersvold, Denmark. Photo by Jette Salling

"I see this school community as a center for humanity. I hope we can help radicalize many young people to fight to end poverty. We are not in the vanguard of starting a revolution but when it does start, I hope we will be one of many oases for people fighting against capitalism and imperialism," Gert Tjoelker tells me during a break in his long day at the Traveling Folk High School (DRH), at Lindersvold School Center, located in southeast Zealand, Denmark.

This property was a manor from 300 years ago when owned by a rich man noted for his warrior killing ability. A century ago, wings were attached to the main building to house a boarding school for "underprivileged children". Some rich like to have the image of being "charitable" by using a small percentage of profits extracted from "their" workers. This charity donation can then be recuperated by not paying the equivalent in taxes, which means less state support for ordinary people's needs.

The boarding school housed children, who were cowed by bullies at school, or who were otherwise socially ostracized – for obesity, for example – for a 10-week vacation. *"Julemærke Hjem"* or Christmas Brand Home, they were called. People of good will sold Xmas seal stamps to collect money to help pay for this charity.

The Traveling Fok High School has been at Lindersvold since 1994. Currently there are about 50 residential students, both in the Teachers Group-run traveling school program and others in special care and educational circumstances, plus day school children ages 6 to 15 in primary and secondary classes. They are bussed daily to and fro.

Lindersvold is an international learning center that emphasizes community development and non-traditional pedagogy. The schooling includes the big issues of our time while preparing students to assist community-driven projects in Zambia, Malawi or Mozambique. The teachers believe in combining hands-on training with theoretical knowledge. They believe that living in a community builds a foundation for working with vulnerable youth and with sustainable development. The school is run by staff and students. All chores are organized within the collective.

Surroundings are beautiful. The buildings are well kept, generally. Residents take care of a garden, 15 hens, tool shed, and sports center with machines and weights, which is also used for putting on plays, plus the living quarters. Besides the main kitchen-dining hall, the special students (ages 10-17), and adults (ages 18-30) in boarding care have their own kitchens, music/TV living rooms. Ping pong is a popular game here. And, as at Tvind, there are Zimbabwe sculptures.

Gert was born in the Netherlands in May1970, just six weeks before the first traveling school was started in Tvind. Even though Gert only got to know about the school's existence in 1997, he likes the fact that they have more or less the same age.

"I had two lovely, supportive parents. I was raised outside a small town. My father was a mechanic in a sugar factory for 46 years. My mother took care of us three kids, dad, and the home. They were traditional folk, reform Christians, regular churchgoers. Few of the kids in my youth were Christians. I began wondering why I was the only one who would get to go to heaven," Gert says.

His world was a workers one, in which they lived in small houses, and heard trains whizzing by.

"We kids had fun playing. I was active physically, and good at studying. Everyone worked hard. It was a healthy life but I got to feeling isolated because of the religious cleft."

Lindersvold school community garden is under expansion. Photo by Jette Salling

"In school I was doing fine. I did well in physical sciences but decided to focus on social science in university. I wanted to understand people; what makes the world tick. At that point, I viewed religion as too unscientific but then what is the meaning with life.

"Studying at Utrecht University was exciting at first. I had a romantic vision of university life, that it would help me understand the world through studies and investigation, that it would help me discover the truth about things through the scientific method. But I got disillusioned about that as it seemed that most students were more interested in getting a career, and teachers and professors were more occupied about promoting themselves and quarreling with one another," Gert recalls.

Upon graduating with a masters in social science, Gert got work with troubled youngsters. He even tried getting a job in a juvenile prison, but management didn't see him as tough enough. So Gert found volunteer work for a while with Moroccan street kids in the city. Then he came across an ad about the Traveling Folk High School at the One World Institute in Norway.

"I was leery about traveling to Africa and helping people. I wasn't sure if we would really be helping, or if we would, in old colonial style, just be helping ourselves. You know, Holland has had its hand in that. But I got convinced about the sincerity of this program and decided to do the 14-month program with six months in Zambia. I worked in a warehouse for seven months to pay for the education and trip. In April 1998, I began the study period," Gert explains.

"It was most demanding, both the studies and living at school with other students. I wasn't used to living a common life surrounded by team mates 24/7. The studies were political and historical, a lot about African history and we also studied and discussed the question of who is ruling the world and what are the forces that shape the world. It was quite enlightening!

"The program was similar to what we now have although we have developed our curriculum. I think what we have now is better in explaining the connections between the big issues in the world of today – capitalism and its neoliberalism, causes for global warming and climate change, and the daily struggle poor people have. Fighting shoulder to shoulder with the poor can be done with more quality and depth when supported by a critical understanding of the world. There are so many actors claiming to help the poor but in reality they are part of the 'Aid Industry'. This special industry manages to profit from giving to the poor with funds from states and governments, which, in many cases directly undermine the productivity of the people in the receiving country," Gert analyses.

When Gert took the DRH education, he traveled with eight other development instructor (DI) students to Zambia.

"We were five in my team in a HPP [Humana People to People] child aid project with different productions. I was organizing and supporting the organization of preschools. Some of my team mates were in gardening and farming," he says.

"As a preschool instructor and organizer it was not always easy to convince parents about sending their kids to the preschool. It was a real question for them how their kids could benefit from schools if all what their children were going to do was the same as them: work the land. What could they learn in a preschool about that?

"We had many meetings, many connections with ordinary people. That is a great aspect about HPP: to meet people where they are and get into consensus with them. It took some time, but finally the decision was made to build preschool classrooms and many children partook," Gert recalls.

"Alienation is a big issue for me, and it hits citizens of this world differently. The exploitation of us in the West is quite a different character than that of poorer people, for example for those living in Zambia's countryside. While we in the West are caught up in consumerism and individualism – and we behave as if this system has something good for us in store, even though we might not agree with it – I met many people in Zambia who had no money whatsoever. It seemed they were completely outside the capitalist system. They lived in small communities in subsistence and coexistence with each other and nature. Our alienation is an estrangement from each other and from nature. Their alienation was not like that. It was more expressed in their wish to marry a white person and escape poverty. Since they know their lives are a struggle, they also know that they need each other and understand the basic struggles of life. In many ways they are not as alienated as we are. It was a pleasure to talk with them, to discuss life with them, because they experience it so differently than I did," Gert philosophizes.

Another example Gert offers about the differences in alienation and his pleasure in meeting people in Zambia occurred in instances of walking city streets.

"Maybe you've seen those very well dressed people walking in Western cities who are too busy and important to take any notice of you. I have been fundraising in those cities, and those busy people were hard to stop and talk with. But when I was in Solwezi, Zambia, and I saw such a business man, perfectly dressed and looking very busy and important – and immediately I thought about those types in Scandinavia – this black Zambian looked me directly in the face and gave me the biggest smile as wide, open and honest as the smile of a kid. Wow! How unexpected, such a contrast to what I was used to, and how nice to meet such a man in his suit," Gert says joyfully.

When the student-teachers returned to Norway their next schooling period was to do the "journal".

"The idea of the journal is to gather the results of our work and go out to meet the European public, to tell them about our experiences doing this work and life in Zambia. For various reasons, I didn't feel I had accomplished enough with the preschools to go around telling others about it so I decided to take part in producing a theatre play, 'Three Penny Opera' by Berthold Brecht. Once we were ready we took it to Tvind to perform in the annual summer theater competition," Gert tells me.

Gert had been thinking about being a teacher in the Teacher Group community and following this summer performances, he joined the TG. He first taught at the Traveling Folk High School in Holsted from July 1999 until moving to Lindersold a dozen years later. At Holsted he met his companion to be, Tina. They now work together at Lindersvold. He still teaches and she is the principal. They work closely together and have two children, a daughter, 12, a son, 10.

"I love teaching. Being a teacher with young adults is such a challenge. I mainly teach at the Traveling Folk High School but have taught special schooling for troubled youth. Teaching, learning, working, living and eating together, creating a community environment without ruling over anyone or looking down on people is a challenge in this world filled with competition, individualism and hierarchy.

"The normal education mission is to keep students misinformed about how the real world functions as a part of capitalism. We are not supposed to understand how things really work, how decisions are really made and for whose benefit. So that is why we run the traveling schools, to make sure that those who join with us learn to understand how the world functions, and do so in such a way that they get encouraged and enabled to do something about that.

"My time in Zambia got under my skin. It really taught me some essential things in life. The accident of birth – in one place one is born with white skin privileges; others are born with darker skin and thus disadvantaged. The injustice of life fostered by racism and capitalism. The roots are greed. We in the West are still living on the wealth stolen from those we colonialized. And so many in the West don't want to know about that, and in this way we brainwash ourselves. To change the world for the betterment of all means to invest in creating a different system. This made me decide to teach people to become aware of these discrepancies.

"My passion of teaching adults all these years is closely tied to my own learning to understand how the world is screwed together. And every time I understand more there are my students to share it with and they share what they know with me.

"All this injustice in our societies; the lies our politicians tell us; the disappointments, frustrations, illusions. It is chaos! But it is only chaos as long as we don't understand. Once we learn to see what it is all about, so it is not chaos, as such, but a system called capitalism. That is what understanding is all about. One can know all the letters in the alphabet and still not know how to read and write.

"Understanding this actually brings pleasure to one's learning! The great American scientist Richard Feynman talks about this in his book, 'The Pleasure of Finding This Out'."

A teacher colleague of Gert's has been listening. Alex Benesch is from Germany and speaks Danish and English perfectly. He loves to talk about politics and history. The three of us discussed this "battle of ideas", which Fidel Castro initiated as part of a national debate dealing with social and economic policies in the early 2000s. This concept was a response to the collapse of the Soviet Union and the isolation of the socialist state of Cuba. Contrary to traditional Communist parties holding state power in various parts of the globe, Cubans argued that the social process – ideas included – must not be subordinate to the economic process but intertwined. Fidel and other leaders hoped to convince young people to reject seeking consumer capitalism, and to win them over, or back to, the fellowship common economy, i.e., to socialism.

"It is ideas that light up the world, it is ideas, and when I say ideas, I mean ideas that are just, ideas that can bring peace to the world, and put an end to the grave danger of war, or put an end to violence. That is why we talk about the battle of ideas." Fidel said in a May 26, 2003 speech.

Gert's take on this is that Teachers Group schooling must be based on a "battle of ideas" and not any economic doctrine or authoritarian approach.

Alex took the necessary teachers training program at Tvind (DNS 2001-5 team) and has been a teacher since. He now teaches at the day school where there are 15 students to seven teachers and assistant teachers. Each student has his/her own needs evaluated.

"These kids lacked care, and some were abused. We teach what they would get in the regular public schools but we do so child-by-child instead of as a classroom unit, in part. Our students are divided into three age groups: 6-9 year-old (1st-3rd class); 10-13 (4th-6th); 14-16 (7th-9th).

"In addition, we teach practical things that many children get in a 'normal' home: how to cook, learn about hygiene, what nature is all about. We take tours in nature. We also introduce them to various kinds of music, to theater plays, to sports, the garden, chickens; we go fishing. We reject the 'organized boredom' prevalent in most regular schools," Alex asserts.

The schooling entails assisting the children to find inner strength, a sense of self-worth. Dancing, listening to classical music (and other kinds), reading and writing poetry are useful in this regard. Teachers hope that by introducing the older children to what is happening in the contemporary political world, in context with history, that they will not only become more knowledgeable but that they will become curious, interested in other people and not only their own navel and rings in noses.

I saw a rehearsal of the current play underway by the older students. Three teenage girls and a boy got dress up in prince and princess costumes. They were quite capable of letting instructor-director Alex know what they thought was the best way to do things.

We were five at the dining table where I sat with Alex that day, all from different countries: England, Sweden, USA, Cameroon, Germany. After lunch, a German student told me that she had come to this school instead of staying at the German university where she had been. "There when one took exams you weren't to write your name but rather you had a number. Here, everybody knows me as Annica, and I don't have to wear high heels and lipstick."

CHAPTER NINE
Student Fatima

***Fatima Gueye at Lindersvold Traveling Folk
High School. Photo by Jette Salling***

Fatou, as Fatima Gueue likes to be called, is 22 years old and has come from Senegal to Lindersvold's Traveling Folk High School for the 10-month course.

In the first three months, students prepare for six-months in an African country, studying its history, culture and politics. They also study global affairs, political science, international and economic development. Historical materialism is presented to the students as a method of analysis in contrast to metaphysical idealism, which claims that society is shaped by ideas rather than a material-technological basis. This approach avoids facing up to how colonialism, capitalism and its imperialism dominate the peoples of the world, creating divisions and violent conflicts, bringing us to this state of permanent war.

Students also conduct investigations about the local people and poverty in Lindersvold's area.

When the students return from Africa, they evaluate their experiences and present what they can to European audiences. The schooling costs 2700 euros ($3000) for enrollment and the whole process, including traveling.

I met Fatou towards the end of her preparation period before traveling.

"I came here with my husband, Mano. He had been here several years ago, but soon after starting the education he had to leave. When we got married in Senegal, we decided to move to his country before making our way here," she tells me quietly as we drink coffee in the school's café.

Senegal has more than a dozen ethnic groups and languages. Berbers from the north settled there a thousand years ago and brought the Muslim religion with them. Portugal occupied the country from mid-1400 to mid-1600 when the French kicked them out, and then ruled for three centuries. Despite five centuries of European domination by countries immersed in the Catholic religion, only three percent of Senegalese are Christian, one percent still practice animism, and 96% are Islamic, mainly Sunni, as is Fatima. The Republic of Senegal was established in 1960.

Mano (Manuel), 44, is from Seville. His skill is network engineering. After working in Spain for a time, he wanted to travel and ply his trade. He worked in the UK, Czech Republic, Ivory Coast and Senegal where he met Fatima. He spent two weeks with her at her family's house in Dakar. They live in the Pikine district of the capital.

"My family was sometimes poor, sometimes not so poor. My father was a tailor but died young of asthma. My mother worked at times, coloring clothing. My brother also died young, of malaria. There was no money for him to be in a hospital.

"My parents had tried to pay for my education in a private school. The public schools are terrible. There can be as many as 130 pupils in one class with one teacher. How can you learn anything?

"My parents were often late with payments. An administrator would come to class and tell everybody who had paid and who had not. It was so humiliating. We often only had rice to eat, and nothing for breakfast. I stayed at relatives houses a lot after my father died."

Fatima is still very thin. She may be so, partially, because she is a fast runner and had been a clothing model.

"As soon as I could work I got a job as a receptionist, and could send some money to my mother. I was always bothered by the pollution everywhere. Most everybody throws plastic and any trash just where they are, on streets, beaches, out of cars and buildings. The government does nothing. I wanted to do something about this. I thought I could be heard if I were known, so I began modeling clothing. In 2016, I entered competition to be Miss Pikine and won. I talked publically where I could about the need to stop polluting the world, about the simple need for trash bins. Nobody took me seriously even though our beaches are disappearing because of severely polluted water."

Once in Spain, Fatima modelled for a time while Mano was busy filling out a myriad of forms to get governmental approval for his wife to live there.

"When Mano told me about this traveling school, I saw the possibility of learning something I could bring back to Senegal to help my people, so we applied. We've decided to take the trip to Zambia. The other team has three people. We will be in different projects.

"This schooling is enriching. I've learned so much about the world of politics, and about how community collectivism can empower people. Many Humana People to People projects [HPP] are improving people's lives, and making local governing more possible. It is encouraging knowing that little Cuba, for instance, has survived the world's biggest capitalist country's blockade. We must all learn to resist these big governments and huge corporations," Fatima asserts gently.

"And today, colonialism in a new form is dominating my continent. The liberation movements have been basically overthrown. Some of this I knew, but here we get to understand why and how they re-dominate us. In the government run schools we don't get to know about this.

"I don't know just how we are going to get our freedom, a true democracy with people decision-making. All of what we can see is based on greedy capitalism. More and more people just think about themselves. There is so much selfishness. It is quite sad. I don't know about us humans. Maybe even if capitalism were to disappear, maybe be overthrown, the next generations might want it again. We can't go back to nature. There may always be people who want power. Maybe alienation can't be eliminated. It certainly can't be until we are all truly liberated. I just don't know about our future," Fatima pauses.

She's looking forward to the Zambia trip in just two weeks. "We will have a guide with us from Gambia. We'll be investigating and working with programs for small children, also a youth club, HIV aid [12% have the disease], farmer's clubs, maybe health care and fresh water projects."

Zambia became independent in 1964. It had been called Northern Rhodesia. Two-thirds of its 17 million people live in poverty; 55% are illiterate. Most are Christians, imposed upon them first by the Portuguese and then the English.

Fatima is good at languages. Her first language is French. She also knows one of many ethnic languages, and she quickly learned Spanish the year she lived there with Mano. She picked up some English and has nearly mastered it in her time in Denmark where she is also learning Danish.

"I hope that in Zambia I can help develop preschool projects. When Mano and I return, and after bringing our experiences to other people, we might go back to Africa and work in education. We'll see. No doubt, though, I will continue this kind of work."

People's Exam 1

I was invited to be an observer-critic of the team's first exam. There are four women and one man – two Spaniards, one Argentinian, one Italian, and Fatima.

Their large classroom includes a library, chalk board and projector, large working table with computers, world map, and plenty of sitting places for an audience.

In this examination, the students have prepared an individual and collective presentation of what they have learned, especially concerning Africa and Humana People to People. They use a big screen, projector and power point technology. They read a bit of text, even a poem or two.

Carolina, from Argentina, begins: "We start with the principle of solidarity humanism: none of us is alone." She presents some of the various school's history, how Tvind helped created HPP.

Manuel picks up from there, showing with illustrations and text how Teachers Group helped fight (without armaments) with Africans against apartheid and colonialism, and partook in some of the first post-liberation schools, community and child-care and health projects.

Pilar also from Spain concentrates on the epidemic diseases especially in sub-Sahara, and how HPP has helped with treatment and prevention.

Franziska from Italy presents a picture of action groups in African communities that decide how to tackle major problems such as: providing a balanced and adequate nutrition for children, assuring that drinking water is healthy, how to prevent sexual diseases, and other problems. She did so without reading from texts.

Fatima takes on the agricultural programs, the Farmer Clubs. She learned something few of us know: 80% of the world's food is produced by small farmers. The mass media always tells us how we need the gigantic agro-industry firms like Monsanto, Kellogg, Dow – those that kick the small farmers off their land, forcing many into committing suicide, all the while they rape the land, polluting it and our food.

The observers found some confusion with statistics and unclear or unstated sources. Walter from Cameroon pointed out that in eastern and southern Africa 70% of the land is still owned by white people, most of whom were part of the colonialization. Their land is usually the most fertile, too.

Someone made the point that there should be better coordination in "spreading the news" when student-teachers return to interact with European audiences. Overall, it was a wonderful presentation, and showed us how much vigor these students have.

Related DRH Schools

Lindersvold Traveling Folk High School has sister schools have similar curriculums, and it is planned to make them the same.

> One World Institute in Hornsjoe, Norway:
> https://www.oneworldinstitute.eu/
>
> One World Centre in Dundee, England:
> http://www.oneworldcentre.org.uk/
>
> Richmond Vale Academy in Saint David,
> St. Vincent and the Grenadines:
> https://richmondvale.org/en/
>
> One World Center in Dowagiac, Michigan:
> https://oneworldcenter.org/

This latter center has a 30-year history. Its director of instructional research and development, Trine Wendelboe, traveled to Tvind last May to participate in the Peace and Justice Conference. https://www.peace-justice.org/; https://www.counterpunch.org/2019/05/24/denmark-peace-justice-conference-based-on-activism-in-many-countries/ Wendelboe, who is Danish, has worked at the Michigan school for 13 years. "We focus on the American peoples' struggle to simply survive the system while we also fight with the poor in other countries, especially in Africa. Americans live with capitalism on steroids. There, hate is 'groovy' and it has a voice in the White House," she told the 200 conference participants.

Wendelboe spoke of the Native Americans' struggle to prevent their land in the west from being taken over by oil and fracking companies. Her school is located in eastern US where the Pokagon band of the Potawatomi people has its headquarters. Most of the 25,000 Potawatomis live in the west, however, and many are under attack for their land.

"The capitalist system is based upon dividing people, and on polluting not only the planet but also our minds. They use myths like, 'everyone can be a success if they work hard enough'. They are masters of manipulation, of anti-democratic laws, such as the recent anti-American law allowing police to lock up people in secret military camps within or outside the United States."

Dividing people is also a part of the capitalist system in Denmark, albeit not so crude and extreme as in the United States. But that separatism is absent in the Teacher Group-influenced schools.

"I am surprised that I can feel at home here," Fatou says, smiling. "I didn't expect that. I was nervous about how I would be seen, if I would be accepted. It's not immediately easy living with people from so many countries with different backgrounds and languages. Nevertheless, it seems that we all learn to control negative emotions, and be less individualistic, helping one another. In fact, I feel part of a family. This will help me throughout my life, I'm certain of that."

CHAPTER TEN
Student Mihaela + New Teacher Greta

*Mihaela in Mozambique during her traveling
high school work-education.*

Mihaela Ungureanu is from Romania. Nearing 30, she looks like a teenager. Nevertheless, she obtained a bachelor-of-arts degree and then worked three years in the food industry.

"I didn't learn that much in school and I didn't feel good at work, didn't really feel good about myself. I had to get out of that state of mind so I looked around for some volunteer work with people, and came across this Traveling Teacher High School (DRH). I chose the 24-month program rather than the 10-month one. With the longer program, one works to pay for the schooling, which is also part of learning, as well as doing studies and the eight-month traveling. I joined up not so much to 'save the world', as to 'save myself,'" Mihaela says frankly.

I met Mihaela just a day before she was to travel to a few cities in Europe bringing to the public what she saw and learned in Africa. This two-month period is followed by taking the Development Instructor (DI) exam. Many of

80

the students do not come back for that, neither did Mihaela, as few employers think the exam is of value, few, that is, outside of several African countries.

The curriculum is based on looking at the "human condition" and putting solidarity in action with those who Frantz Fanon called, "the wretched of the earth".

"During the first year, I worked with needy youth from six to 18 years of age. It was hard work but a good year. We DRH student-teachers worked alongside Tvind DNS [Necessary Teacher Training College] students, all of us guided by trained teachers. These special problems these kids had were all new to me. I learned to open my mind," Michaela says.

While they work, the teacher-students also learn from the DRH texts books and digital information about: world history; the forces that shape the world; the big issues like war, poverty, climate change; getting close to the lot of the poor; new technologies and the future of technology; organic farming for food.

"It was a difficult period, too," Michaela admits, "because we student-teachers were not all together most of time, and communication was not ideal. We worked three-fourth the time and then were at Lindersvold one-fourth the time. I had doubts about continuing, and most did drop out, but I found that I wanted to realize something in my life. I needed to be responsible for myself. It made me stronger to overcome challenges."

Enrollment fee for this education is 2,100 euros ($2325). The tuition, room and board, and traveling costs are paid by their work during the first year.

The student-teachers make teams of three. Each team can choose to travel to either Zambia, Malawi or Mozambique where there are projects and indigenous schools associated with Lindersvold through the Zimbabwe-based Federation Humana People to People. Mihaela chose Mozambique along with two other DI student-teachers. They lived side by side with African students at the One World University. Europeans who come can often help their fellow African students with English. DIs-in-training are told that they will have to be innovative and cannot expect that everything will be prepared for them. Part of the training is solidarity work and traveling to other places in Mozambique or a neighboring African country with indigenous students who study for four years.

"We were to travel one month on bikes and sleep in tents," Mihaela tells me. "But because there was a poor infrastructure, we mostly traveled by mini-bus. We looked into agricultural projects and some schools but we didn't feel we were of much use. When we got back to OWU our local DRH guide was too busy to help us so we were on our own. We were like swimming around for some months, trying through trial and error to find out what we could do.

"Finally, we found that we could renovate a community building. For the last two months, I helped build a playground in a community pre-school. We used mainly sustainable materials, and got some donations for food. We lived very simply, and I learned how much water means to the entire world. I now take short showers having learned to bathe with 2.2 liters of water in Mozambique.

"We were to travel again but a big cyclone prevented us. So we investigated some Human People to People education and health projects. Overall, nobody told us what we could do. We had to find out on our own. This was quite different from what the other team experienced in Malawi where there was better organization and discipline," Michaela continues.

"The program could have been better. In the end it was a soup of circumstances. We need to look deeper into our experiences. No doubt we had profound experiences yet we wanted to realize more concrete results, more activities with the kids. Much of the time I didn't know what I was doing. I nearly dropped out but for my own integrity, I promised myself I would not. Now comes perhaps the hardest part: how to transmit all this to other people in Europe. And then to find out what I want to do with my life, what kind of work I want to do and where.

"I know also that when I get home my family and friends won't really listen to what I experienced, or care about how the people live. Not too many white Europeans are interested in others' lives, or how so many are *forced* to live."

"What did I get out of it all?

"I understand a lot more about the world. I also learned not to see only the bad: the poverty, the wars, the racism and nationalism. There are good things in this world, and I can see some. I've come to appreciate my family and friends more.

"Looking back, I see we did do something useful after all. I can feel a bit proud realizing that small things matter, that I can be happy without having comforts all the time. Furthermore, being happy is not everything."

#

Greta Lupieri was the only DI student who took the exam and graduated the 24-month course out of the original group of 16 people. Their key teacher, Gert Tjoelker, spoke to me about this phenomenon.

"Most of the European students who come for this schooling want to be heroes. We tell them that the African project and school leaders are in charge and have much on their hands. We are their Western partners and they and we agree that part of the schooling focuses on students learning on their own, in certain respects. That means our students should observe the environment, get to know the people and in that way, find out what they as Western student-teachers can do to best assist.

82

"In September we are starting a new 10-month program with ten students. In February 2020, we'll have a new 24-month program. Out goal is to have four DRH teams a year and one 24 month."

Veteran teachers say that the traveling part of the program can be improved. One of the problems is a lack of experienced teachers. When they have had enough teachers, one travels with the DIs-in-training as is done in Tvind with the DNS classes.

Like Mihaela, Greta was older and more educated than most when they join DRH schooling. At 27, Greta had a masters degree in political science and economy from a university in her country, Italy, when she found Lindersvold School Community on the internet.

"I wanted to do something to improve peoples' lives, especially those who Europe had treated badly. Unlike some of my teammates our threesome that went to Malawi had more positive experiences. We learned from Malawians the usefulness of Humana People to People projects. I worked on building preschool classrooms and could see how helpful they were, especially for mothers. Malawi folk helped me acquire a universal vision."

Greta Lupieri at Lindersvold garden.
Photo by Jette Salling

When Greta returned to Lindersvold she took the final exam and was invited to become a member of the Teachers Group. She was pleased, especially with the offer to lead a new project, "fighting global warming" at Lindersvold community campus.

"I made a five year commitment, the first two years as coordinator of a new climate project here. We will form a team for at least nine months to make a large, more vital organic garden, and have more hens and other domestic animals with better conditions. We will soon have three people to help. They are taking courses at St. Vincent's school," Greta tells me.

"You know, as an Italian [temperamental, expressive, ed.] it was easier for me to be in Africa than here in Denmark. Here individualism reigns; there the community took center stage. But some of our neighbors here are OK. There is a Steiner school nearby and they accept us. And I've made contact with a neighbor who is a biodynamic farmer. He is friendly and helpful in giving me advice. So, maybe the climate project will grow into something positive."

Lucas Traveling Folk High School teacher at Lindersvold café-library sits with Zimbabwe sculpture.
Photo by Jette Salling

Lucas Ehrenhaus is Gert Tjaelker's new co-teacher in the 10 and 24-month Traveling Folk High School (DRH), in Lindersvold, Denmark.

Lucas, 43, is the epitome of Teacher Group's internationalist character. He was born in Belgium of German parents, in 1975. He describes his roots.

"On my father's side, my great grandfather, a *régisseur* [stage manager] touring Germany, becomes aware of the advent of war. He takes his two kids to Argentina because there is a past Jewish relative in the family. One of the children marries my grandmother. She is Austrian of Austro-Hungarian relatives and a forlorn father who was a tobacco farmer from the US. Married in Argentina, my father is a German-Argentinian citizen. On my mother's side, her father is a first generation ex-pat from Scotland living in Argentina. My parents meet at school and marry. The Argentinian military dictatorship's repression pushes my parents to Belgium. Four years after I am born, the pressure subdues and my family moves back to Argentina."

The military had overthrown the government of Isabel Perón. She had been former President Juan Perón's wife and vice-president from October 1973 to July 1974 when he died. The army was displeased with her. It had previously overthrown her husband, September 16, 1955, in a coup d'état during his second presidency.

Another German family that fled the rise of Nazis in Germany was the Kissingers. The son, Henry, became President Richard Nixon and then President Gerald Ford's Secretary of State. This Jew advised Argentinian fascist military coup makers to murder its active opponents, many of whom were Jews. Upon the coup takeover, March 24, 1976, they put President Isabel Perón in prison. She was released after five years and exiled to Spain. From the start of the military junta until it lost the war with Britain over ownership of Malvinas/Falkland Islands, in 1982, it "disappeared" and murdered around 30,000 people, plus torturing and imprisoning tens of thousands more. All this was encouraged and directly aided by the CIA's "Operation Condor". *(See note at end of this chapter.)*

Another of history's ironies is that during Juan Perón's first presidencies (1945-55), he granted asylum to thousands of fleeing fascists from Italy and Nazis from Germany despite the fact that Argentina had more Jewish citizens than any other Latin American country, and Perón was the continent's first president to recognize the State of Israel.

Lucas has led a restless life.

"I went through different phases in which school was not quite remarkable. I started work at around fourteen. School faded in my view. I travelled in Argentina with schoolmates and changed schools several times, ending up at night school," Lucas tells me.

"In 2001, I traveled to Spain and knew I wouldn't return. I was there 15 years. Spain was good and bad for me. I was a waiter, barman, driver, delivery man, sales man, sales technician, shop and ware house supervisor or manager. The economic crisis hit hard but I got a deal with my boss and was on the dole for 22 months. Very grateful to that because it allowed me to travel, learn and become an English teacher, like grandmother and my mother. I taught for five years in various of the biggest companies in Spain: Iberdrola, KPMG, Ericsson, Zurich, AXA, Oracle, and a couple dozen more.

"I saved up for a year to work in a ski resort in Lake Tahoe, California. I had a blast for that season   though this didn't allow me to grow. That triggered me to look for other opportunities, but it was not very easy, so I decided to direct my attention to helping other people. I found the link that yielded the DRH Norway program [The One World Insitute]. I thought of using my teaching ability 'fighting with the poor', and bought a one-way ticket just to make sure I wasn't going back. I didn't want another cultural shock. You know, 'burning down the bridges'."

To pay for the schooling, travel and room and board, he worked at a natural reserve hotel in Norway and then for several months collecting and sorting used clothing in Denmark.

"Sorting tons of clothing is hard work, physically, and also psychologically being with new people, mostly kids. I was also driving a truck to collection centers gathering these clothes, and then sorting them. It caused me to lose my excess fat, and I'm glad for my body change.

"This 'learning by doing' was a real challenge – a positive one in the end. Not only working together but eating together, doing practical chores and living collectively forced me come over my natural laziness and social individualism. I've learned skills, especially social ones, that I otherwise never would have. And I'm glad not to be drinking. I was a heavy drinker for two decades. So I have grown," Lucas says.

"The studies were also an eye opener. Normal education doesn't show you how the world really works; this program does. We learned history, politics, cultures through real people, and without indoctrination. We students become our own motivators."

Africa and Muslims

"My first experience with the Muslim culture was in Morocco. The initial shock was the toilet behavior. I was able to learn much about Muslim culture from Muslims themselves as I had found a family to host me through 'couch surfing'. The man of the house worked with goats and his daughter was my guide. She worked for women's rights, and she helped me during my two weeks of investigating the area, the people, their religion and culture. It was a rewarding experience."

When Lucas team got to Guinea Bissau traveling on local buses, they met heat waves and poverty.

"Guinea Bissau has a lot of poverty but that didn't shock me as I had seen a much of that in Argentina. Its soil was similar too: bright red, rough earth. Its language, Portuguese, is similar to Spanish. So, I was alright there.

"Another DI student and I worked at the vocational school in Bissora, which Humana People to People [HPP] had constructed."

Bissora has 11,000 residents, and they have benefited from HPP development projects since the 1980s. A maternity hospital was also build there.

"My job was basically to identify problems we could fix. There were many: infrastructure, constructions, renewable energy, and agriculture. The first we tackled was the lack of water for a Farmer Club orchid. The idea was to collect rain water. I made a plan and a budget. It takes a long time for HPP sponsors to approve specific projects and budgets. Once a project is completed by both local people and, usually, with DIs and DNS student–teachers [The Necessary Teacher Training College], it is independently run after a year or so. Any further work is through African DIs from the nationally affiliated schools where Teachers Group has had a hand," Lucas explains.

"Sometimes when funding ends, the project peters out. The headmasters are usually in the TG but many of the local teachers are not. Not being a part of the common economy-space-distribution that is core to the Teachers Group's sense of cooperative responsibility, many of these teachers just see their work as another job, and sometimes they don't grasp the whole picture," Lucas continues.

"Not all HPP projects employ TGers, and not all of them see the whole picture either. Some TGers are stationed at headquarters not at the local projects where problems crop up that require skillful and quick attention. Learning how to run everything, how to develop and maintain what is produced, requires education, funds and recovering from colonialization and neo-colonialization.

"You do what you can, and a lot of the European student-teachers drop out of the program, frustrated. When we returned and took what we could to other Europeans, there weren't many of the original class left. In fact, I was the only who took the exam and graduated."

Lucas and Teachers Group

"I was offered a job teaching the DRH in Norway. I felt close to the community life. Putting our earnings in one pot, so to speak, is liberating. Just having some pocket money while administrators and accountants pay our bills frees us to do what we want: teach," Lucas says contentedly.

"I was a co-teacher with two 12-month classes in Norway, one after another. One never became well integrated, and several students left early. In the next one, I led a team to Columbia and Ecuador. It went smoothly.

"Then a new 10-month DRH program started here in Lindersvold and I was offered a co-teaching spot. This program will probably be a standardized one. There are some aspects that are a bit traditional and fewer choices for the students to make, but the same vision and materials are used. One problem that needs correcting is that some of the material is not well written in English.

There are so many people with varying original languages and from different cultures involved in shaping our materials that they end up not being coherent enough. There are too many grammatical errors, misspellings and too much poetry, I think. Yet to correct them will take a lot of time and patience.

"This job is really a non-job. It is a way of life. There is one line – no pyramid – in the Teachers Group. We're all on the same platform and decision-making process. Sure, there is always somewhat of a hierarchy given that many have long seniority and others are new, but there are no bosses. Everyone is a worker. Yes, there is peer pressure yet free will is endemic in TG. We learn to live in a community, taking common actions, learning new cultures, languages, traveling. Together we can tackle some big issues, which we cannot alone. Maybe we can help show people another way: that this unfair system is not necessary."

"I like the common responsibility. The TG has a council, which meets weekly to make common decisions. Sometimes TGs from many schools meet in a larger council. That is also something that the conference center in Mexico is used for.

"I made a two-year agreement and was welcomed in the community. In reality, I can leave whenever I want to. I have become detached from stuff and appreciate a Zen-like mindset. I can always travel on bicycle or hitchhike. Money for cars is not necessary. I'm satisfied with TG."

Once Gert and Lucas current 10-month class left for Africa, Lucas was offered a job in England CICD (College for International Cooperation and Development). It is a DRH School in Hull. He is collecting and packing used clothes. The perennially restless Lucas moved again.

"There is always a big need for extra hands. I am also helping with building team rapport with the new DI students, participating in common actions such as building weekends where all neighbor schools participate in painting, fixing, installing…the usual," Lucas concludes.

#

Note: The Junta collapsed soon after the war, in 1983, and an election was held on October 30. Lawyer-statesman Raul Alfonsín was elected president by 52% of the voters. Below can one read the role Henry Kissinger played in convincing militarists to kill radical activists and unionist workers. Also read how the CIA set up "operation condor" to "eradicate" radical opposition to US-supported militarist-dictatorial regimes in several Latin American countries.

https://www.theguardian.com/world/2003/dec/06/argentina.usa

https://www.globalresearch.ca/operation-condor-and-the-united-states-torture-death-squads-and-echoes-in-the-new-millennium/5672589

https://www.latinamericanstudies.org/chile/operation-condor.htm)

CHAPTER TWELVE

Former Teacher Sven Erik

Sven-Erik Simonsen decades after teaching as a member of Teachers Group.

"If I were not organized in my party [The Communist Party], I would still be with the Teachers Group [TG]," Sven-Erik Simonsen tells me in his and wife Helle Brunn's apartment, located in a Copenhagen working class district.

Sven-Erik's parents were farmers in the Jutland mainland. Born in 1951, he was one of six children on the 12-hectare farm. They just managed to make ends meet. Sven-Erik grew up like most "ordinary" Danes with one difference: he refused "military duty". Sven-Erik opposed war, especially seeing what was happening to the Vietnamese people brutally subjected to USA mass murder. The Danish law allows conscientious objectors to do civilian work instead. This liberal law inadvertently allowed Sven-Erik to get introduced to the burgeoning left-wing of the late 60s-70s. His first job was in the post office in Copenhagen. Now he would learn from protestors.

"I joined demonstrations against the Vietnam War, and the one against the World Bank's exploitation of especially poor people in 'third world' countries," Sven-Erik tells me.

"That is when I met my girlfriend," he says, smiling at her sitting on the sofa half-a-century later.

Helle's brother had taken the DNS (The Necessary Teacher Training College) at Tvind and she was with the DRH (Traveling Folk High School) in 1974-5.

Helle joins the conversation.

"In 1974, I was in Portugal during the DRH traveling period. It was a useful trip in many ways. One lesson was, we learned what is means to fight against military rule and be able to win through a peaceful transition. It increased my curiosity about the world," Helle says cheerfully.

In 1980, Helle was a UFF-HPP activist (Humana People to People) and helped build a school in just liberated Zimbabwe, former UK colony "Rhodesia".

Helle Brunn in Zimbabwe during a recent return visit to projects she had worked with.

Sven-Erik had taken up social pedagogy and was working with marginalized and abused youth.

"I became involved in social pedagogy work as a substitute for military service. Later I was at the same institution. I learned by doing, the attitude I later developed at Tvind Small Schools," he says.

"I decided to continue working with troubled children while Helle was in Zimbabwe. When she returned, I joined the Teachers Group [TG] for three years. They accepted my work experience as a social pedagogue. Tvind had several large sailing ships used as maritime colleges. Some still exist. I took two long trips with youth and young adults [16-36 years of age].

"These ships as schools had great success bringing many young people out of their doldrums, helping them find self-esteem and become self-sufficient. *(See Note 1 at end of this chapter.)*

"On one trip across the Atlantic, on "The Big Bear" [Den Store Bjoern], we were four sailors – two were in the TG – three teachers and about a dozen youths."

At the time, this three-mast schooner was the largest wooden sailing ship in Denmark. It was 37 meters long and sails up to 30 meters high.

"Sailing long distances is a fantastic structure for social pedagogy. Many of the students were alcoholic or drug dependent; many had been or still were criminals, and some quite violent. We teachers sometimes had to restrain them physically to stop their violent behavior, something that is up for discussion today as a necessity amongst teachers and public school administrations," Sven-Erik explains. "Really though, there were few such conflicts.

"On a ship, there must be discipline and order. We were able to accomplish that. They had duties like everyone else and they were performed. We'd be at sea for weeks before landing for some days. We made stops for supplies, to see some of the land, and do some learning investigations. We did this in Portugal, Brazil, and Caribbean islands.

The good ship, "The Big Bear", built in 1902 as a stationary radio and light signal ship. Converted to a schooner in 1980, until recently used as a small school for troubled youths.

"They also studied even though they were generally anti-intellectual. We had a library on board. Imagine, some of these kids read books such as 'The Fishermen' by Hans Kirk," Sven-Erik says.

"The Fishermen" is still Denmark's most read novel after nearly nine decades. There is no key character rather collective characters of five families of fishermen, who are deeply religious and intolerant although quite solidarity with one another. Intolerance clashes with openness under the pen of this lifelong communist author. Kirk, who was also an attorney, fought the Nazis underground before Danish police arrested him in 1941. He was imprisoned until 1943 when political prisoners got word they were to be deported to Germany. Kirk was among those who were able to escape. He died in 1962.

"We teachers taught what we knew but also learned from our students – we all became wiser about the world. It was a real victory for our pedagogy that many of these hard-nosed youth learned to read and even enjoy good books, meaningful ones at that," Sven-Erik emphasizes.

"You know, The Establishment likes to harass Tvind and TG, contending we were a cult, authoritarian, doctrinaire, and what not. Yet TG has had colossal effect on the Danish educational system. Politicians and the mass media, however, don't want to admit that. Before Tvind public school education was traditional, top-down taught and boring. TGs schooling backed up the natural rebelliousness against this, the university student uproar. Since then more student input has been allowed. Traveling is also a part of public schooling now. The idea of living and working as a cooperative has also been accepted."

Sven-Erik lived at the Tvind school community when not sailing. Both he, and Helle, who had been there the decade before, witnessed some of the times' leftist extremism as many flaunted traditions.

"Some rebels actually wanted us all to wear the same clothing. Not only were there extremist vegetarians, but some were so avidly anti-tobacco that they would come to where smokers slept and crush their cigarettes. And for a time, there wasn't much respect for professional skills. But that behavior and attitude didn't last long. People either grew up or left," they tell me.

Sven-Erik became a father, twice. After three years teaching and member of TG, he settled into an apartment with Helle, joined a communist party, and got a fund-financed job as a social pedagogue or rather a community-activist.

"Together with a small group, I started a 'community center' where we tried employing some of the TG ideas in a poor working class area – working with children, youngsters, adults and elderly."

"I worked at a special school and still used TG methodology. Some of the 'client' students were working class others were lumpen proletariat. Some of the latter were members of the 'Green Jackets' [Young skin-head racists inspired by Nazis, who painted swastikas in public places.]."

"Imagine! We arranged a trip with them to Turkey to meet and play soccer with Turkish youth. The skin-heads learned first-hand that Turkish people are not dumb swine. They had a good time in Turkey and enjoyed meeting Turkish people. That experience really rocked with their previous negative attitude. It was not, of course, a complete healing but it made a fundamental impression on many of them."

Later Sven-Erik worked with second hand clothing at UFF between 1989 and 1993. This was as a "non-member" of TG. As others doing this job have told me the clothing collection, sorting and marketing is very hard work, and rewarding knowing that some of their sweat gets a school built somewhere in the world for children who might otherwise never learn to read and write.

Sven-Erik was never very active trade unionist, but nearly his whole life he has been a union member, also when he was in TG. He denies that TG should be hostile to trade unions.

"We were and I think they still are in favor of all kinds of organizations that unite and strengthen people and can be used in the struggle for bettering lives and the world," Sven-Erik tells me. "Yet from time to time, there have been conflicts. TG members are dedicated more to the work than to sticking to 37-hour workweek. That has provoked conflict in some cases."

A couple years ago, Sven-Erik traveled with Helle to Zimbabwe to see what results came out of the funds raised through the collection of second-hand clothes – and not least to visit the projects where she had worked in 1980/81.

"We were encouraged by what we saw. Clearly, many people have a better life because of these projects," Helle says. "The key to our work is, of course, the end product, but it is also that people are aided in solving problems that they can. We are accepted by local people, because they realize we are not 'luxury' Europeans. We sleep beside them, so to speak, often in tents, and not in hotels.

"Many more people have acquired education because of TG work. Terrible diseases like AIDs have been reduced, and there is more aid for people with the disease. TG and HPP, as a whole, are appreciated also because the local people take part in decision-making, and continuing the projects once set up. HPP projects don't only deal with the material aspects of life but also about building organization and consciousness. This adds a promising perspective to the projects. People become 'armed' to solve any problem or challenge in that way."

So why do nearly all left groups and political parties turn their backs on Tvind/TG?

"It's true that most of the left, especially 'progressives', do not support them. Our party always has. During the 'special law' period and since, we have supported them through our newspaper, and since it closed down through our net-newspaper. A number of our party-members were students at their schools back in the 1970s and early 80s," Sven-Erik explains.

"Teachers Group is too collective, though, for most people, including most leftists. Furthermore, the times have changed, regressing to individualism, liberalism. TG decision-making process of consensus is hard to take as well. Its high degree of collectivity and discipline scares most people, though that is not the case in Africa where TG/HPP have projects, and where hundreds and thousands of people join with the Teachers Group."

"Yes, and in hard times so many people in our part of the world go toward the right when it really costs something to be in the left. Moreover, the witch hunt against Tvind and the Teachers Group takes its toll," Helle adds.

"Teachers Group has done so much already, I don't know what more one could ask of them. They were really tenacious to fight back against The Establishment, and go out in the big world to find new means of continuing and growing," she summarizes.

"In the early days, Tvind/TG was a great catalyst for global and humanistic consciousness, for organizing, for bringing people of all kinds close together. They broke through the limits and contributed ideas and experience to help change society. Today, these extreme me-me times have pushed that out of most people's reach and thought," he concludes.

Special Schools for Troubled Youth

Sven Erik has had quite a lot of experience with these special, "small" schools before and after being in Teachers Group. He says teachers do not beat the youth but do sometimes have to restrain them by holding them down, as he had to do a few times on the maritime schools. The issue of using restraints, or violence, has popped up in Danish and English media recently. Not all of it is Tvind or Teachers Group related but some is.

Last summer, the Norfolk, England regional newspaper, the "Eastern Daily Press," wrote that eight former students at the TG-led small school in Buxton, Red House, had alleged they got "broken bones [from] being restrained and being beaten up. Some said other students had beaten them and even raped some, but that the teachers did nothing about it," wrote Tom Bristow, July 26, 2019.

The reporter stated that some cases had been reopened even after police had investigated allegations in the 1980s-90s, and as late as 2009, without raising any charges. One man, however, did successfully sue social services, in 2001, for sending him to Red House. The school was closed down in 1998.

These allegations were picked up by some Danish media, especially the net newspaper, www.kommune.dk, which covers Establishment politics. Its reporter, Ronja Pilgaard, wrote several pieces. In one, she interviewed a main defector from TG, Steen Thomsen, who had been principal at a sister school, Winestead Hall, 1991-98, just before leaving the TG. He had been a member since 1977. Upon leaving, Thomsen wrote a strong critique against what he viewed to be authoritarian and cultish behavior at Tvind when Mogens Amdi Petersen was present. Nevertheless, he told reporter Pilgaard that he had never had a student transferred to his school from Red House because, as one boy claimed, he had been raped by other students at Red House.

Thomsen said that while another TG member, who had been principal at Red House, was "rough" with students at small schools, "one cannot speak of a violent culture," Pilgaard wrote. She also reported that Thomsen said that most often "students [were] glad at being at the small schools."

So what is the big fuss all about?

A current long-time TGer, who also worked at these schools in England and is now in Denmark, explained that there are changes in rules in the English special school system, which allow for old cases of alleged mistreatment to be re-investigated and if found to be true the people hurt can get monetary compensation from municipality funds. So, some lawyers place ads in local newspapers encouraging adults – who were children at these schools, and claim they were abused – to come forth to file cases for money. If they win, lawyer-client split the sum.

Danish journalists asked the leader of a social oversight agency what she thought of these allegations in regards to TG-led schools in Denmark. The social oversight chief responsible, Ulla Bitsch Andersen, replied, "I have difficulty in seeing how we could conduct sharper oversight with these places. This also has to do with very old relationships."

Two years ago, Andersen was approached by Denmark Radio (TV) journalists with similar claims about one of 37 special schools where TG has teachers and some members on the executive boards.

The television program "Revealed" alleged that at Nakkeboelle Fjord small school several students and a few teachers, who had been fired by the leadership, claimed that many cases of violence, which were noted in the daily logs, were not reported to the proper authorities as required.

Andersen's extensive report on the matter was made public. It states that 14 investigating visits had been made to this school over a three-year period, half of which were unannounced. Investigators found some critical matters and the school leadership acted upon them. The social oversight report states that nine "injunctions" it had made were taken seriously and corrected. This included changing directors. One complaint not related to internal relationships, which was corrected, was that rents for buildings and facilities were artificially high. They were reduced by 80%.

Helle says that the media finds it easy to attack Teachers Group in relation to problems at small schools, but the government is making it difficult for all small/special schools to survive with its continual funding and personnel cutbacks. Yet there is always enough money for war weaponry.

Banana Kingdom Denmark

September 2, the day that Yankee President Donald Trump should have been in Denmark, between 1200 and 1500 demonstrated against US-Denmark wars, to tell both states: "Yankee Go Home", "Take Back Denmark's

Sovereignty". This was the largest anti-war gathering in a long time. Some people came out just to protest vulgar Trump, or to oppose planet pollution, and other issues.

Trump cancelled the trip because the Kingdom of Denmark, as the Queen and her politicians call it, would not sell the real estate capitalist its colony island of Greenland. I suppose Trump figured that since Denmark had already delivered its foreign policy sovereignty to "the greatest country in the world" two-three decades ago that it would be willing to sell him Greenland, so that the US Military Empire could have more military bases with nuclear armament there. This logic was premature.

On the same day we demonstrated, Denmark's "social democrat" war minister "coincidentally", sent four F16 war jets Denmark had bought from Trump-land years ago to "protect" the Baltic from the big bad bear.

Denmark's government also announced it was buying top-notch sonar, so it could play along with its Big Daddy when they go searching for allegedly Putin-run submarines and, of course, there would be more funds for NATO. Not least, Denmark's war minister announced that she would assure that her elite killers – Commando troops and Navy Seals (Jaegerkorpset and Froemandskorpset) – will be used all the more to protect Denmark against Russia. She announced this without stating what the threat was, but assured us that this "fellowship" with NATO and the US will "be effective when there is need for it."

Big Daddy got what he wanted without wasting his time and tax money with a trip to Banana Kingdom Denmark. Three days later, on Flag Day, the media published photos of mothers and fathers in military uniforms pinning war medals on 700 children chosen that day, because their parents were or had been sent out to do their duty.

On the following day that the feminist prime minister (Mette Frederiksen) and feminist war minister (Trine Bramsen), alongside the male feminist secretary of state (Jeppe Kofod), announced the same number of soldiers (700), coincidentally, would be sent to war zones or potential war zones: Syria, Africa, the Baltic for starters. The explanation for this escalation was "Russia's aggressive behavior in the East", and that there were terrorists in many countries. The government will also sail Denmark's largest vessel, a frigate, to assist a US aircraft carrier group. Denmark will assist US in its sanctions and rattle sabering against Iran. Denmark already participates in war missions in Afghanistan (now for 18 years) and Iraq, and "defense" of Kosovo and Estonia. They will continue to do so.

"We have once again been asked to contribute to peace and stability out in the world's hot spots. I am proud of that," asserted the "Social Democrat" war minister. *(See Note 2 at end of this chapter.)*

One would have thought, Banana Kingdom Denmark had certainly proven itself, yet once again, to be the best possible warring ally the US

Military Empire could wish for, but no, these contributions to US/NATO war-making were not enough.

During this week of jingoistic swashbuckling, 40 war ships with 4,500 marines from 16 NATO countries docked in Copenhagen's harbor. The government also extended its territory reserved for war game maneuvers from 6000 to 14,000 hectares. Finally, for now, the Royal Family's main home, Amalienborg Palace, will be blocked off from all traffic by 1.2 meter tall bronze bollards. Christianborg's Parliament was so blocked off earlier but with mere 85 centimeter tall granite balls. Again, we must be in constant fear of terrorism, but not their own.

I mean, what more could the US Military Empire ask of its little Viking ally?

#

Note 1: Tvind schooners have sailed hundreds of thousands of kilometers, and have had three wrecks, only one with the loss of lives. Eight members of the TG died in a Gale in the North Sea near the English Channel, on February 1, 1983, when the "Activ" capsized. It had recently had a leak repaired. http://www.jmarcussen.dk/maritim/skibsliste/side.php?id=

Note 2: On an historical note, we should recall that there are two direct opposite definitions of "fellowship" (or "unison") for social democrats and real socialists. During the days leading up to the Russian Revolution, the Russian social democratic party had two factions, "Bolsheviks" and "Mensheviks" – the former wanted socialism (leading toward a stateless communist society), and the latter opted for "social democratic" capitalism – a la Bernie Sanders of today. The split ended with the Russian Revolution attacked by armed social democrats and their allies, the aristocratic "white army", and its allies the US, six European states and Japan. Before the 1917 revolution, German social democrats had gone along with the bourgeoisie's insane world war, and social democrats have since followed suit in scores of countries and in hundreds of wars.

CHAPTER THIRTEEN

Songwriter-singer, activist David Rovics

David Rovics has been a troubadour on the road for quarter-century. He comes to Denmark nearly every year usually more than once. I met him again last summer at the Teachers Group school-care home at Hellebaek on the east coast of Zealand. He was their Hellebaek Café barista and caretaker for two months. His wife and three children came also from their home in Portland, Oregon.

David has associated with Teachers Group (TG) for a decade. He plays and speaks as a musical-activist-organizer at some of their arrangements. Here is his song about Café Hellebaek:

https://ru-clip.net/video/5aMSzxppK5Q/cafe-hellebaek.html

We talked for hours at Hellebaek, mostly about Teachers Group and the Tvind school community. He first met Mette, Hellebaek's director, at a spring 2009 concert where he played on the occasion of Pete Seeger's 90th birthday. (See Story 2 for more about Hellebaek.)

"Mette is a longtime member of the Teachers Group and had helped build Tvind's windmill. She, her husband Lars Peter, and other Tvind folks were involved with the COP15 [UN Climate summit] protests a few months later, and I was, too. They organized a concert tour for me of, I think, 17 different spots throughout Denmark. So, it was soon after we first met that I started seeing quite a bunch of them, and meeting lots of other folks associated with Tvind from around Denmark and the world," David tells me.

David Rovics describes himself as an anti-Zionist, anarchist and wobbly – member of the Industrial Workers of the World (IWW).

Born in 1967, his parents were liberals, classical musicians and educators. When he was young, they moved to Wilton, Connecticut, a conservative, Christian town. In 1985, Rovics enrolled at Earlham College in Richmond, Indiana but dropped out and moved to Berkeley, California. He worked as a cook, barista, secretary and typist, while performing on streets, subways and in small clubs and bars. In the early 90s, he was a full-time busker involved in leftist counterculture. He shuns commercial business and is an indie (independent) musician. Although most of his work is distributed commercially, he makes all his recordings available free as download files.

Rovics sings resistance songs in the tradition of his favorite political folksingers Pete Seeger and Phil Ochs, and their mentor Woody Guthrie. He often speaks about his role as a resistance activist musician. In one fundraising concert, in 2002, for the Baltimore Chapter of SUSTAIN (Stop U. S. Tax-funded Aid to Israel Now), he told the Baltimore Indymedia: "U.S. governments' foreign policy represent U.S. corporate interests", and "the U.S. government does not like democracy either at home or abroad."

Rovics also writes a newsletter and essays often published on counterpunch:

https://web.archive.org/web/20150111112500/
http://www.davidrovics.com/bio.php, his website with photos
https://davidrovics.bandcamp.com/

… and …

https://en.wikipedia.org/wiki/David_Rovics.

"An organizer, just like a musician, can be motivated by both the love of music as well as the desire to use music as a tool for radicalization and popular education," David recently wrote:

https://www.counterpunch.org/2019/09/02/remembering-mitch-podolak/

David feels close to the Teachers Group schooling work and knows about the witch-hunt.

"Of course, anyone's first association with those involved with Tvind, especially if it includes a web search of the name, will give you a whole load of stuff to read and attempt to sort through, including accusations that the founders of the organization are cult leaders and criminals. The nature of the accusations are complex, which also makes them difficult to even discuss, let alone refute. The biggest problem in Denmark with Tvind, at this point, is that most people start out with a completely inaccurate and negative view, so just getting to '0' takes a long time. Tvind members, and even just people like me associated in some way with Tvind, get tired of this," he says.

"My own experience has been that some of the most knowledgeable, caring and shining souls I have ever met have been Tvind founders, members of the Teachers Group, very much including Mette and her late husband, Lars Peter, but also many others too numerous to name. They are all over Denmark, also in the US and other countries where I travel. Wherever they are, they're doing great work of many different kinds. What interests me as much as their work is the experiences so many people have had, living for extended periods in many different countries, and traveling widely in many different ways, especially by bus. The stories are endless and fascinating, if you can get people talking, which isn't usually easy when they're Danish – and they don't drink alcohol!

"Mostly Teachers Group avoids the media, which is fine, given how the Danish media treats anything related to Tvind. I wish they might focus more on creating their own media, which is what I've tried to do in my own small way by writing, '*The Biggest Windmill in the World*,' and various podcasts and other things…

"I've sung for lots of people in the Necessary Teacher Training College program in many parts of Denmark and other countries, but not in a way that it's been part of their official program of education (as far as I know). It seems that everyone who has been to Tvind ends up hearing my song about the windmill, though."

It was in the 1970's, the fuel crisis had begun
The choices were presented to us as if we had none
Leaders of industry said they could solve the problem
By mastering the power of the radioactive atom
Some folks in western Jutland got a notion in their heads
They thought there might be something they could offer up instead
A few hundred people gathered in a little place called Tvind
And declared their will to harness the power of the wind
We're gonna build the biggest windmill in the world (2x)

There were many who said their science wasn't sound
That such a mighty windmill would simply topple to the ground
Some of them were scientists, the vast majority were not
But they knew with years of effort you could do a lot
Word about the project spread far and wide
A hundred thousand visitors came to help and to advise
Until one day these windmill builders drove in with a crane

And lifted up their giant wings with a mighty chain
We're gonna build the biggest windmill in the world (2x)

When Tvindkraft was completed it reached up to the sky
Its wings churned in the air at 54 meters high
The critics all fell silent, no one now was jeering
As even industry agreed this was some damn fine engineering
The wind regaled Jutland from the north Atlantic sea
As it was seamlessly converted into electricity
It was power for the people, leukemia for none
When they declared in Denmark just south of the midnight sun
We're gonna build the biggest windmill in the world (2x)

They gave away the patents, they said knowledge should be free
And their plans were copied by a new-born industry
Soon Denmark would be known as the windmill-building nation
And it all started with some hippies at the Tvindkraft power station
Debates were held in parliament about which way things should go
Build a nuclear reactor, the majority said no
It could have gone quite differently – in much of the world it did
Except for those in Ulfborg who said we're getting off the grid
We're gonna build the biggest windmill in the world (2x)

From "Letter to My Landlord", released March 28, 2016:
https://davidrovics.bandcamp.com/track/the-biggest-windmill-2

I wrote about the windmill. See the preface and an article about Tvind's Peace and Justice Conference.

http://ronridenour.com/articles/2019/2505--rr.htm

Tvindkraft website states: "Tens of thousands of people flocked to Tvind during the construction of Tvindkraft. Without their advice, encouragement and practical assistance the windmill would not have been … a true windmill of the people."

https://www.tvindkraft.dk/en/history/why-the-windmill-was-built.html

Helge and the Windmill

In the same week I spoke with Rovics I also came across Helge Knudsen, who had helped build the windmill. He was at Tvind in 1974-5 studying in an experimental high school program. Helge was not part of the regular Tvind school community but lived with his classmates close to TG people. During his time there, he was called to military duty, which he refused. Helge was able to do civilian work instead, and that allowed him to work on the windmill for three months with two other military objectors.

"My year there was rather one-dimensional. We students did most of the schoolwork ourselves, that is to say, we taught ourselves the program. Most everyone was involved with preparing for the windmill construction," Helge tells me.

"Amdi [Mogens Amdi Petersen] was an unbelievable guy. He had overwhelming charm. He always had the last word, yet he was open to discussion and there was free exchange. He lived in a house and had a car but it was used collectively. I even used it once to drive to the dentist."

Tvindkraft still standing tall.
Photo by Jette Salling

"Working on the wind turbine was extremely exciting, a great learning experience. We had to teach ourselves, really, new expertize. There were scientists or educated engineers with us too. One of the key engineers left for some reason. Some TGer went to Holland to fetch him back. There was some tension about that, and he didn't seem happy either, but he was important for the work and did it."

Helge had mixed feelings about his stay there. He felt that unions and communist parties were not appreciated, that there was too much concern about getting money and too much control.

"They did have a lot of good ideas, actions, and projects. There were many good people, and some extremists too. Why, I even met somebody who thought jazz music was imperialistic."

"I thought just to educate people wasn't enough. Tvind wasn't working class based, but the atmosphere helped me become a revolutionary. When I left, I took work at a major ship-building yard and joined the union," Helge says. "I lived in a collective and became a Marxist." Soon thereafter, he joined a communist party, and is still a member today in his mid-60s.

Back to Rovics

"The overview, in terms of the work these people do in so many countries, Africa and elsewhere, is fascinating. When I'm at Tvind, Hellebaek or other of their school campuses I'm constantly meeting people who are leaving or coming back from months in far-away countries.

"I'm more personally familiar with the day-to-day operations at the Hellebaek social village. I would have loved to have been here when it had a bigger school environment involving these brilliant radicals who form the Teachers Group, but I wasn't around to see that. What I have seen is how they work with troubled youth and people with various issues and disorders. The success they're having is obvious, and it also seems obvious that part of that success is just the fact that the residents who are getting different forms of treatment are also living in community with various others: teachers, teacher assistants, and folks who have been in what we could call the long-term, informal Artist-in-Residence program. The time we spent at Hellebaek and its café was a lovely experience of community living," David concludes.

One of David's most loved songs, and my favorite, is "We are Everywhere":

https://www.youtube.com/watch?v=n8j8BmgeYLA:

When I say the hungry should have food
I speak for many
When I say no one should have seven homes
While some don't have any

Though I may find myself stranded in some strange place
With naught but a vapid stare
I remember the world and I know
We are everywhere ......

CHAPTER FOURTEEN
Student Maksim

*Two generations united in admiration for Che Guevara
and his quest for the "new man".*

In the photo, I hold in my right hand a small red carton box with Che
Guevara's face on it. On the right side is a little steel handle that one winds to
hear the instrumental music, *"Hasta Siempre, Comandante"* (Until Victory
Always, Comandante), dedicated to the iconic revolutionary.

Cuban composer Carlos Puebla wrote this piece shortly after Che "disappeared", in 1965. What happened was unknown, but Cubans generally thought that he had gone to fight for liberation somewhere else. What happened came forth after his assassination, in Bolivia, October 9, 1967. Che had taken a few hundred guerrilla-trained Cubans to the Congo – now Democratic Republic of the Congo – to aid the native guerrilla uprising against the US-Belgium backed dictator, Joseph Désirí Mobutu. After many months without progress, Che sent his men secretly back to Cuba where later Che would lead another group to start a guerrilla war, in order to free Bolivia. *(See Note 1 at end of this chapter.)* Here are stanzas of the universalistic song:

> *Your revolutionary love*
> *leads you to new undertaking*
> *where they are waiting for the firmness*
> *of your liberating arm*
>
> *We will carry on*
> *as we followed you then*
> *and with Fidel we say to you:*
> *'Until forever, Commander!'*

Maksim Ivanov gave me this revolutionary gift in a gesture of comradeship after he had read my book, "The Russian Peace Threat: Pentagon on Alert", which includes chapters on revolutionary Cuba during Che's time there. Like so many other Lithuanians one meets in Teachers Group (TG) school communities, Maksim (22) learned of Tvind's DNS program (The Necessary Teacher Training College) through its social media outlets and word of mouth.

"I was interested because I realized that governments want people to obey, and so its public schools assist. Tvind is obviously a problem for governments because the teachers and students don't drink alcohol or take drugs, rather they discuss real politics and real history," the lanky youth tells me.

"DNS courses show us the problems people face due to the system's control, and encourage us to do something concrete against it. So, we must be 'bad guys', who steal money from their treasuries that they take from the people.

"When I understood these negative perceptions of Tvind and the TG it made their schooling all the more exciting," Maksim says, grinning.

"You can see how much good is going on here in the community. Our togetherness keeps us going and it doesn't matter what 'they' say about us. However, it does take courage to go through this process. We do have resistance from many ordinary folks, who don't accept that there can be other ways of existing, of acting and be happy doing so."

Maksim takes me on a tour of the bus, which he and other DSN 18 (2018) students rode in during the four-month trip to Western Africa (November 2018 - March 2019). There are 16 seats with shelves for computers. Students continue reading texts while they ride, as well as conducting investigations along the way. There are storage areas overhead and under seats for books, clothes, and food. They prepare meals on a fully operating kitchen though without baking possibilities. They use gas to boil and fry food. They transport water for washing clothes and cooking, as well as bottled water they drink when the local water is contaminated.

Sometimes they sleep in sleeping bags on top of wooden boards placed on the seats, or in tents set up nearby the bus. "We only occasionally eat out in restaurants. Many restaurants in Africa sell food at expensive prices, even as much or more as in Europe," Maksim states.

The former school bus that the previous DNS 17 had bought is about 12 meters long and two meters wide. DNS 18 had 14 students and two teachers, including two who had drivers' licenses.

African Trip

"We began on schedule with a time plan but the bus had different plans," says Maksim wryly.

The bus finally made the ca. 20,000 kilometer tour to and fro but not without several break downs. First, there was a fire in Spain – reminiscent of Simona's DNS 13 bus breakdown in Spain *(see Chapter 4)*. Then a rear axle broke in Morocco.

"In Morocco, most of us had to hitchhike to the nearest town where there were mechanics. They towed it in, but they weren't skilled in fixing this kind of vehicle. Both local mechanics and some of us took off parts and got them welded or replaced as best we could. We were there four-five days. We conducted investigations. Some were easy enough because several local people approached with the idea of traveling with us. Some street kids thought we could help them get to Europe. One of our investigations was about the Moroccan government's hard-handed policies against the Western Saharan people. Some of us spent days with Moroccan families. When the bus could continue, we saw military patrols between Morocco and Mauritania. We didn't do investigations in Western Sahara directly as we couldn't risk getting arrested and deported," Maksim says. *(See Note 2 at end of this chapter.)*

They spent several days in Mauritania conducting investigations into slavery and the Islam religion/culture. Their conclusions were similar to those already expressed by other storytellers in this series.

DNS student Maksim Ivanov in front of the bus he had traveled in to Africa. It has made two such trips.

"I can't generalize about Islam," Maksim says, cautiously, "but it seems that the teaching methodology is to memorize the Koran and other scriptures. Slavery is still extensive and there are activists fighting this."

After arriving in Senegal on a ferry there was another two-day delay for bus repairs.

"On the return trip, we observed elections in Senegal. France is still active in controlling what it can of its former colony. The politician that France backed with money and propaganda won. They paid for a lot of advertising at many places, including at Shell gas stations," Maksim explains.

Obviously former British and Dutch colonialists, who own Shell, help their EU ally. Their opposition in Senegal wanted more independence, including such simple things as traffic signs in native languages, and not only in French. That, however, sounded too much like a threat for more sovereignty. DNS 18 students also learned that the educational system was more France based than natively. They avoided stopping in southern Senegal and northern Gambia, as there were armed conflicts for independence, so they drove straight through to Guinea Bissau.

"Some of our classmates assisted students in vocational schools, with solar panels and Farmers Clubs. Others made investigations about the effects of climate change, which is causing the sea and rivers to overflow onto farming land, causing a decrease in fertile soil.

"I worked in one of the first cashew nut factories in the country. By processing locally, the people earn a greater share of the sales, which otherwise goes mostly to Portuguese and French companies. HPP staff and funds aided setting up this factory. This is one of the most exciting and potentially large local and even national projects," Maksim says enthusiastically. *(See again Simona story Chapter 4.)*

Maksim describes the factory process.

"They now have a nut sorting machine, and a mechanized roasting method. Nevertheless, to peal the skin from the fruit, in order to get to the nut, is still a hard manual process. You use a sharp scalpel knife blade to peal off the skin. Sometimes, it breaks the nut. It took me four hours to get just a soup bowl full of nuts. Native women are faster, of course.

Cashew nut apple fruit.

"Once there are enough roasted nuts, they package them in plastic bags and ship them to the markets. Where I was most were sent to Germany. The local people use the cashew apple fruit for its milk, but this is also exported."

The milk is lactose free with lots of unsaturated fats, proteins, vitamins and minerals, which can maintain a healthy heart.

Maksim also witnessed DNS teacher training that would help rural children. Many schools have been built with HPP aid in remote areas where there had been none. Still as many as 70 students were in primary classrooms.

"We built a fence around one school so that neighbors' animals couldn't get in to eat from the school's garden," Maksim says. "We also made a meeting area from bamboo, and built a clay oven for baking bread. We had learned how to do this from a neighbor. Now, they wouldn't have to travel to market to buy bread and their own would be less expensive."

Before Maksim takes off to Zealand in eastern Denmark where he will work with used clothing at UFF headquarters, he tells me what he has learned and how he feels from his first year with DNS.

"There are clearly two worlds far apart from each other. I can cherish the advantages we Europeans have while feeling upset that Europeans waste 40% of the food produced and bought. This is tragic all the more so when so many people in Africa lack food.

"We DNS students have seen Moroccans wanting to get to Europe simply to get out of poverty and away from violent national problems; Senegalese suffering from lack of basic survival conditions due mainly to Western-caused climate change; people in Guinea Bissau subordinated to a one-crop economy imposed upon them by Western cashew nut consumption; and Western racism and discrimination against African refugees coming to Europe simply out of the need to survive.

"I learned that Africans can take care of themselves without the 'white savior' if only the Western states and their rich people didn't try to re-colonialize them."

UFF and Humana People to People

I saw Maksim a couple weeks later sweating from packing used clothing at UFF-Humana's warehouse. We embraced warmly, exchanged a few words, and he returned to his work while I talked with Else Hanne Henriksen, who directs UFF-Humana's work in Denmark. We had only a short time since she would be flying to Zimbabwe in a few hours. She had partnership visits to projects in Zimbabwe.

"UFF-Humana [*Udlandshjaelp fra Folk til Folk-Humana People to People*] was started by students at the Traveling Folk High School in Tvind, in 1977," Else tells me. "This organization stems from our decision to fight apartheid in much of southern Africa."

Else has worn many hats. She has taught in private and public schools. She has been working at UFF in Finland and Denmark for a dozen years. Else has participated directly in solidarity work by building a boarding school in Zimbabwe right after its independence, in 1980. Much of UFF-Humana's donations go to HPP in Africa.

UFF-Humana are also sending used school furniture to schools in Guinea Bissau and Zimbabwe through funds from Recycling for Development.

"I helped organize some people into collective production and distribution activities, and assisted with gender equality. It has been a real pleasure to return for visits, to see the positive results of these endeavors. Why now it is progress that primary and secondary children no longer must sit on the floor," Else Hanne concludes.

Ever since the Danish government began its investigations into Tvind, and related schools, the special law and court cases against TG members, UFF-Humana has been under a magnifying glass for possible misuse of money acquired, in part, from the sale of second hand clothing. Some authorities contend that some of the money goes to "Tvind" and not to the humanitarian projects for which it collects and sales clothes.

The mass media from time to time still sends suspicious messages to the public about UFF-Humana and Tvind. Yet monetary accounts are separate from any Tvind-related activities, and their books are open for regular official inspections. UFF-Humana has not been charged for any illegalities.

As I write this, I search for media stories alleging TG sins, and here pops up one of the latest. On June 21, 2016, the "liberal" "Politiken" daily ran this cynical headline about UFF-Humana: "Money to foreign help: From People to People or from People to Tvind". There wasn't even a question mark nor was there any evidence of such slander in the article written by Peter Sinnbeck.

Interestingly, just under this cynical piece was reference to a "Politiken" headline of February 2, 2012: "2000 tons unusable clothing: Danes use recycling bins as trash cans". Unusable clothing that charity groups would have used for poor people included panties with holes in them, clothes smeared in grease and rotten food....

**UFF has 850 such used clothing containers
spread throughout Denmark.**

Last year UFF-Humana and its partners throughout Europe and the US collected 138,000 tons donated by 20 million people. These clothes were bought by 10 million Westerners, and 14 million people in Africa and Central America. This humanitarian work has created around 15,000 jobs, more than half in the latter continents.

The clothing industry accounts for 10% of global CO_2 emissions, and the fashion industry produces 14 times the clothing needed for every person on earth. The conclusion is: discarded clothing that is useable should be used, especially for people who cannot afford new clothes, also to diminish waste and planet pollution.

What follows are some figures and descriptions about what HPP is doing and what it has achieved.

Figures are taken from the Federation Humana People to People 2018 annual report.

"The report provides an insight into the work of the Federation and our 30 member associations over the past year, including our commitment to impact, accountability, and transparency in all our work. In 2018, working across five continents, members…implemented projects in sustainable agriculture and environment, community development, health and education in 1,134 project units. These projects reached more than 9.5 million people and represent a vital contribution to reducing the effects of poverty and supporting communities to address some of the world's most significant humanitarian and development challenges," wrote the new federation chairman, Snorre Westgaard.

"The Federation for Associations connected to the International Humana People to People Movement was formed in 1996 by the then 16 national associations in Europe and Africa…

Since 1993, HPP, "More than 42,000 teachers have been educated in Mozambique, Angola, Malawi, Guinea Bissau, Zambia, D. R. Congo and India. The teacher training colleges have DNS programs spanning from one to three years, and all except those in India are boarding schools."

In India, HPPI has been active since 1998 and currently has projects in 14 states. It works with 2000 organizations in 60 development projects. Last year DNS (Nett in India letters) taught 6,500 teachers in five states. Government subsidizes the education.

One of HPPI's current activities is assisting women out of dependence upon patriarchal oppression. "Humana Microfinance empowers economically disadvantaged women in India by providing access to entrepreneurship loans [which includes support for] training skills, and functional and financial literacy. The group lending model distributes risk and guarantees loan repayment."

An Indian medium, CB Bureau, wrote an analysis of HPPI, "Humana People to People India: Spreading themselves too thin?" in November 2018. I searched what I could to determine how accurate and objective this medium is. I cannot vouch fully for it but the bureau does seem to seek balance and fairness in its reports and investigations.

It states the following about itself: "CauseBecause intends to contribute to the understanding of the professional reality of NGOs as well as how diverse corporate groups align their corporate social responsibility strategies with communities and their issues at large." CB has 120 reporters, stringers and editors in several states. I could not determine how it is financed, nor did it respond to my query.

I excerpt from it anyway: https://causebecause.com/humana-people-people-india-spreading-thin/6232

"Operating since 1998, HPPI works on numerous programmes for poor and underprivileged communities in rural and urban India. Partnering with international and national organisations including the government, it has implemented more than 140 projects across the country. Currently, more than 50 projects are in the states of Rajasthan, Haryana, Uttar Pradesh, Madhya Pradesh, Bihar, Uttarakhand, Jharkhand, Telangana, Tamil Nadu and Delhi, reaching out to around two million people annually.

"HPPI's projects cover a wide range of intervention areas: education, CDP (community development project/programme) and livelihood, health, environment and microfinance…

"The number of people impacted through HPPI's numerous interventions is extremely impressive, if even half-true. In 2016–17, the numbers were more than 2 million beneficiaries through 60 development projects and 40 microfinance branches. In all, 1.2 million women were empowered through its many projects and more than 60,000 women got access to microcredit. Moreover, 40,000 children and 5,000 teachers have benefited through in-school interventions."

CB criticism of HPPI appears credible given what I deduced from several readings of both HPP reports, and elsewhere, and correspondence with it.

"While HPPI has been doing some much-needed work in multiple areas, questions remain on its many claims about the impact of its programs. While a few assessment reports are available online, considering the sheer number of projects it is involved in, such reports should be the norm rather than an exception. The annual report will also become a much more meaningful exercise if it includes data on impact and gaps. Assessment reports should also have information on initial feasibility studies, benchmarking and goal-setting…and follow-up studies to understand the long-term impact…It is not known if external agencies have verified these assessment reports."

CB makes reference to the history of accusations against TG-related programs, including HPP, and recommends what it might be able to do to respond: "(I)t could counter such suspicions by releasing comprehensive data on its programs and getting them audited by reputable firms, as it does with its financial statements. The best way to dispel negative perceptions, whether deserved or not, is transparency and accountability.

"Another recommendation would be to streamline the number of projects and areas of operations. Right now, HPPI seems to have its finger in multiple pies but there seems to be little reason to believe that this is a strategy that's working for them. Most of its monetary investments, as well as the better-designed projects, are in education and livelihood and it would be prudent to focus on these areas and do them right. HPPI already has the network and funding, and it makes sense to leverage these in a smart, effective way."

Back to Denmark. UFF-Humana director Else wrote me that Maksim finished his time working with used clothing, and is on a short vacation with his family in Lithuania before continuing his DNS studies. She writes, "We were very glad for to have him."

#

Note 1: The first prime minister following independence from Belgium, in 1960, was the intellectual, progressive liberationist Patrice Lumumba. He was murdered, January 17, 1961, by national rightest forces with CIA and Belgium assistance. The key issue then, as it continues to be, was national sovereignty vs: neo-colonialist control of the Congo's important minerals, among them uranium, which is essential for nuclear weapons. In the last few years alone, a raging regional proxy war has killed over six million people. The US-EU are the profiteering neo-colonialists. The African people the perennial victims.

Note 2. Western Sahara is populated by half-a-million Berbers, mostly. They speak an Afro-Asiatic language, and practice an Arabic-Berber culture. Since the eighth century, Berbers have embraced the Islamic (Sunni) religion without, however, its current fanaticism by many groupings.

Western Sahara was used by the Spanish as a port for slave trade from the 1700s, and Spain officially made it a colony in 1884. During Franco's fascist rule, he granted his ally Morocco control. Since 1973, it has been a disputed land between Morocco and the Popular Front for the Liberation of the Saguia el Hamra and Rio de Oro (Polisario Front), an independence movement based in Algeria.

CHAPTER FIFTEEN
Fighting Capitalism with Capitalism

Teachers Group (TG) did not want to own anything, but it was forced into the capitalist economy by the system's politicians once they had closed down so many TG-run schools and thus their revenue. TG would not give up. It started businesses. One of its members, Simon Lichtenberg, came to Tvind with his parents when he was seven. After being raised in Tvind-related school communities, he studied business at Harvard Business School. Simon moved to China and studied at China Europe International Business School, and Tsinghua University. He is fluent in Chinese.

Denmark is known for its design qualities, lamps and furniture. Lichtenberg founded the Trayton Group to make furniture. He franchised the Chinese Bo-Concept, Danish lifestyle furniture. Trayton specializes in leather upholstery (Simon Li) and Kvadrat fabric for seating and curtains. Their products are sold widely including in North American and to the world famous Swedish firm IKEA.

Today, Trayton has three factories in Shanghai and Zhejiang employing 2000 workers. They are paid the going Chinese wage plus paid vacations, paid sick leave and health insurance. In 2008, it was China's largest furniture producer.

Trayton annual revenues surpass $100 million. Some profits went to install rooftop solar panels and lighting in Shanghai streets, in 2012. Since Lichtenberg is a life-long member of TG, some profits end in their common "yellow bucket", just like when they started.

http://www.traytonfurniture.com/gro_introdcution01.htm

http://www.chikungunia.com/business-academy/10-things-to-do-in-shanghai-by-simon-lichtenberg-simon-lichtenberg

Treading backwards to go forward

Now, the main question for anti-capitalists with regards to fighting capitalism with capitalism (FCWC) is: should there be limits; can there be limits; ends and means? A TG veteran told me that they did make one restriction: there would be no marketing speculation, no stock ownership. Good. Is that the only limit?

The key intellectual leaders of the young revolution in Russia were Vladimir Lenin and Leon Trotsky, both of whom wanted to immediately start forging a socialist economy, a permanent revolution and spreading this to other countries wherever possible. This was too ambitious, perhaps. Yet we will never know, because, of course, the internal and foreign opposition prevented it from succeeding through making war, economic sabotage and blockades.

Wisely enough, Lenin launched the New Economic Policy (NEP), in 1922. It was to be an economic system including "a free market and capitalism, both subject to state control", while socialized state enterprises would operate on "a profit basis".

The NEP was deemed to be necessary after the Russian Civil War of 1918 to 1922, in order to boost the economy, which had been crumbling since 1914. Soviet authorities stepped back from the complete nationalization of industry, established during the period of War Communism of 1918 to 1921, and allowed individuals to own small enterprise, among other concessions.

Lenin used the expression, "One step forward, two steps back" when explaining internal contradictions and diverse lines in his own party at an earlier time in the Russian Social Democratic Party (1898-1912).

Cuban revolutionaries were also ambitious in the beginning. Che Guevara even experimented with abolishing money, in order to advance socialism to create the "new man". Naturally, the world capitalist class with US military Empire in the lead would not allow such solidarity humanism to exist. However, Che's idea of "mobilizing the masses" with a moral instrument by "converting the society into a gigantic school" did obtain some success – that is what Teachers Group tries, too.

Christmas 1991, Mikhail Gorbachev abolished the Soviet Union with one stroke of the pen after telephoning his good friend, George Bush I. Boris Yeltsin had taken over command of Russia. He stopped solidarity relations with Cuba, after consulting with his comrade Bill Clinton. So, the stalwart revolutionary leader Fidel Castro was also forced to make concessions. He declared the Special Period in Time of Peace given that nearly overnight Cuba lost 80% of its imports, 80% of its exports and its Gross Domestic Product dropped by 34%.

To alleviate the economic crisis, the government introduced market-oriented reforms: opening up for tourism from the West, allowing foreign investment, legalizing the U.S. dollar, and authorizing self-employment starting with 150 occupations.

China, Vietnam, Cambodia had already backtracked on most of its socialist economy, allowing for free market capitalism, even neo-liberalism. In 1992, the Chinese government called their economic reforms "socialist market economy", and learned from Western and Eastern capitalist economies. The state still maintained control over essential resources and infrastructure but new capitalists were permitted to become as rich as under any capitalist system. Socialist welfare was severely cut back. Higher education and health care were no longer fully covered by government funding. China has recently begun to reinstate some of those losses.

What we have witnessed is that no revolution, which wanted to create a truly socialist economy – with the aim of gradually developing full equality and communism in which the state could disappear – has been able to develop. The main reason is that capitalism is still too strong and dominating. Its masters do everything to undermine revolutionary efforts to fulfill the humanitarian vision. Globalization – the fulfillment of imperialism – is the period we all live under today.

So, it is not strange that the Danish state would make it impossible for Tvind/Teachers Group to exist and continue with their anti-capitalism ideology and schooling activities with funds from the capitalist state. They either had to fall in line with the capitalist state, give up, or adopt some method of fighting the capitalist system by using it.

In my opinion, the choice they made is understandable, but they go too far. That is always the dilemma: means to ends. I had the same judgment when I lived in Cuba (1988-96) and suffered along with everyone else through the special period. I use to say, adopting *some* capitalist measures is like being *a bit* pregnant.

Today, the Cuban people, as a whole, clearly want capitalism. They just want to hold onto welfare benefits they achieved during the socialist process, mainly state-supported health care and education. Yet that can be achieved within a well-functioning, advanced capitalist economy as well.

Teachers Group Conference Center in Mexico

"The conference center is the first time we built something for ourselves," Annica Mårtensson, DNS (Tvind's Necessary Theachers Training College) headmaster, tells me.

Teachers Group made the decision to build this center when Denmark began its court case against eight of its leading members in the early 2000s.

"It was a big process to make this decision. We mulled over it and finally decided for it. It was a big investment out of our own pockets and our physical energy and time. Many of us helped build it alongside Mexican workers. And Jan Utzon designed it," Annica explains.

Teachers Group's worldwide conference center at
Las Pulgas del Pacifico in northern Mexico.

"We use sustainable solar energy, local food and materials. We need it to unite our members from around the world. We have many kinds of courses at the multi-purpose conference center. I've been there for days or a week or so, sharing experiences, information and programs. Being there has enormous value for me personally and for my work. It is an energy boost."

It took four years to build the center. By 2008, it was fully operational with several members living there, taking care of it and running conferences. The mass media has widely reported that Mogens Amdi Petersen lives there too. That is not anything that TG members wish to talk about.

According to various reports, including the local official newspaper, "Periódico Oficial de Estado de Baja California", reporting on 22 de junio de 2012, the 800-hectare location houses: a 144-room apartment-hotel for members and guests, five restaurants/cafés, swimming pool, fitness center, cinema, library, several meeting rooms, a large hall, and gardens. According to the official newspaer the cost was reported to be 328, 578, 147 Mexican pesos in 2010 terms. That was the equivalent then of $26 million. That sum, say several TG members I spoke with, is the equivalent of between two and five apartments in middle-class areas of Copenhagen.
https://www.documentcloud.org/documents/2801017-Mexican-Property-Record-SECC-I-22-06-2012.html#document/p12/a289288

Justinas (see Chapter 1) was there for a media course when I was preparing this series. He told me about his experiences.

"We were 48 TG members from several countries sharing our learning about media-recruiting work. It was amazing talking with people from so many parts of the world. Some were DNS students and project leaders from Africa and India," Justinas says.

"There are always fingers pointing at us for having this 'luxurious' center, and noise about Amdi. I found the center to have simple rooms, standard meeting rooms, ample space and a place where we could do our work. It feels like a conference center, period."

Periodically the Danish media complains that "Amdi" should be imprisoned, and that the Mexican center is a product of his ripoff. The Establishment always fingers one leader to discredit the whole lot, and all that they stand for.

Sven-Erik (Chapter 12) looks at it from a global development perspective: "Why should it be problematic that a large organization has the need to meet and discuss their work? What right does the mass media have for its criticism? It was built with TG's own money. I think it is a beautiful example of their hard work and fellowship instead of using private wealth for big houses. It is inspiring for us as is their honest work."

Neither the Mexican local official newspaper or the Mexico government nor, for that matter, the Danish government has come up with any illegalities concerning this center. The center's existence is a useful location made possible by using capitalism to fight capitalism.

While the center may seem luxurious to some, there is no personal monetary benefit in it. Teachers Group members do not get money from this. The mass media does not complain nor do politicians when capitalists like bank owners and CEOs "score the cash register" as the expression goes in Danish. Nor are there slanderous charges against members of parliament, for instance, for taking $106,000 a year plus $25,000 tax free cost allowance from tax payers. Besides the folk pension that every citzen and permanent residents are entitled to, they get up to $63,000 in annual pension once they have been in office just one year or more.

A single person's folk pension is $25,200 annually before taxes. Minimal tax is 38% of income. That comes out to a take home income of $15,600. That is what Teachers Group members get.

The last CEO of the scandal-ridden *Den Danske Bank*, Denmark's largest bank, which is still the bank the government uses, received $2.1 million annual salary plus that much in bonus when he left the post last year. Thomas Borgen was not fined or jailed for being the top leader during years in which gangster-drug dealer money was laundered by his bank. This is one of those banks that has helped rich people hide their money in tax shelter islands, and committed any number of illegalities, some of which are under investigation. There are other banks involved in these crimes but if there is any punishment it is in the form of fines that the corrupt individuals do not pay. No one goes to jail.

Humana People to People Charter

As stated earlier, the Teachers Group did not get into capitalism directly for its own organization until the 1990s, but when Tvind/TG started UFF, in 1977, it began engaging with capitalism to finance humanitarian projects in Africa and India. In 1996, TG helped create the Federation of Humana People to People with 16 national associate member organizations. Two years later, this process resulted in its charter.

"The Charter of Humana People to People is a piece of art. It is an example of how it is possible to write the history of the future. The future of Humana People to People was written down in 1996 and launched in 1998 after a 2 year process, where everyone in Humana People to People read the Charter as an inspiration and expressed themselves in writing and drawings about their dream, vision and plans for the future of their projects."
http://www.humana.org/who-we-are/89-the-charter

Excerpts chosen here show the mixture of using capitalism to assist people out of poverty, and to spread an anti-capitalism understanding, and doing so with a poetic pen:

"When destitution is master, when disease spreads, when suffering walks about the landscapes – naked, free...The dehumanized human being, the dehumanized society must meet The Solidary Humanism. Man standing shoulder to shoulder with all mankind.

"Then we bring food and clothing and jobs to the poverty-stricken...Then we support liberation. We create new locations with new jobs under new conditions. Then we do our bit to get rid of the tyrant...

"Then we unite with the liberating powers of the peoples. Then we organize the right conditions for our own profitable farming...[schools, culture institutions, health care, community care] Then we become native Americans in our hearts and ecologists in our practice...

"Then we become part of the struggle against the plague and the war. We create jobs. We take actions...Then we place ourselves in the line of fire. With our thoughts, our words, our deeds...

"When oppression tortures the souls, we support liberation. Identify ourselves with the struggle. We torment pain until victory...

"The basic ideological battle between fascism, capitalism and communism finally fought to a decisive end [sic ?. ed.], with a multitude of versions of

parliamentary democracy, connected to the free marketplace as every nation's understanding of its economy.

"Humanists deliberated while they saw it happen. Now it has happened. The world will for a long time have to develop within the framework of the parliamentary democracy with a free marketplace. This charter thus accepts these conditions as the framework within which activities of HUMANA PEOPLE TO PEOPLE shall unfold."

OK, that's the decision: fight capitalism with capitalism. Yet on the same page, HPP still hangs on with the vision of socialism – although instead of using that unacceptable term for potential donors, they use "equal distribution" – because they know there will be "more very poor people."

"Thus the policy of equal distribution is still a must for the committed humanist."

After several pages describing how FCWC can unfold for the real benefit of the poor, the holistic minds of these sensitive scribes summarize:

"We have learned from the idea of running a private production company for the sake of profit. We now do so in several efforts, spending the profit according to the articles for the general benefit of our other projects. A growing contribution now comes from this sort of activity. It has been a problem for us to conform to this thinking – we are admittedly [ed.] balancing on the razor's edge – but the future has come to stay and today we clearly see, that more funds will and ought to come from ourselves [ed.] as our own commercial sponsor."

Then a few pages later another contradiction:

"It is our experience that development will have to be taken care of by the powers of the nation. But it is of greatest importance to insist upon and to incorporate the active powers from all us little people...The dangers of development and the risks involved on the road ahead give credit to the courageous and accept the mishaps as an integral part."

They close with remarks to others who struggle for a wider vision than what capitalism has to offer.

"Let us begin by declaring that this organization is not tied to a single issue or single events like wars of liberation, campaign for or against certain political or ecological ideas or other single causes. We do not in any way think ill of others who have chosen to have such ties. We just do not ourselves have any. Live and let live. This organization is tied to the idea of development in the full sense of this concept. In space is means extension into infinity and time never-ending. In effect it refers its supporters to a life as

nuclei of change in service to the forces of change...that changes this world to a better place for all mankind."

Human beings cannot organize themselves without contradictions. The Marxian dialectic is always at play: thesis, antithesis, synthesis. I can only hope that the synthesis envisioned is still one of abolishing capitalism, and there with its imperialism-wars. The very conclusion of the HPP charter makes it clear, clear to me at least, that there cannot be a world that is "a better place for all mankind" as long as capitalism reigns. Only an economy based on equality – some sort of real socialism – can do that.

Humana People to People Under Attack: CIR-Planet Aid controversy

For reasons to which I am not familiar, the Center for Investigative Reporting (CIR) has it in for anything connected to Tvind, Teachers Group and HPP. In the years 2016-17 it wrote several articles and some radio podcasts claiming that these entities were cheating monetary donors by taking money for humanitarian projects, which either were not productive or did not exist, and using donor funds for other purposes.

This is what CIR says about themselves on their website: "Founded in 1977 as the nation's first nonprofit investigative journalism organization, the Center for Investigative Reporting has developed a reputation for being among the most innovative, credible and relevant media organizations in the country." https://www.revealnews.org/about-us/

CIR has a newsroom staff of 56 and 12 in administration and development. Its funding comes, in part, from major capitalist and even fascist-friendly corporations, namely: The Henry Ford Foundation and John D. Catherine T. MacArthur Foundation. In his prime, John MacArthur was the third wealthiest US American. His money came from banking, real estate and insurance. Henry Ford was an avid racist, anti-unionist and a notorious admirer of Adolf Hitler, who had his full portrait on his desk. *(See Note 1 at end of this chapter.)*

CIR's website is Reveal News. Reporters Matt Smith and Amy Walters maintained that the US Department of Agriculture (USDA) should not fund any of HPP projects. The USDA had aided HPP with $133 million over a decade. Most of this went to health, education and farmers clubs projects in Malawi and Mozambique. These reporters went to a few of these projects in Malawi, and came to Denmark to talk with former TG members. http://www.revealnews.org/article/us-taxpayers-are-financing-alleged-cult-through-african-aid-charities/

Reveal News hashed over the Danish government's history of stopping funding and the failed court cases, contending that Amdi Petersen was a criminal. They found a former USDA employee inspector to say that some

Malawi farmer clubs crops "did not indicate a success rate", and he doubted their value, but nothing criminal was determined.

A couple of African TG members complained that their pocket money from the common wages was not adequate to raise their families. CIR found some farmers to say that there was more show of success than actual progress. Two of CIR sources were subjects of criminal actions. Smith and Walters' African co-author had been convicted of two felonies for trying to extract money from someone he threatened to write about negatively.

CIR reporters stated that Marie Lichtenberg is the key liaison person between Planet Aid (HPP) and USDA. Yet USDA was not impressed with these reporters' claims, which they judiciously stated. "To this day, USDA officials say they see nothing wrong with Planet Aid. Reveal sent the Foreign Agricultural Service a letter describing these investigative findings in detail and followed up with a list of detailed questions asking why the agency continued funding Planet Aid despite the warnings of possible fraud. The agency sent back a note saying it takes its project review process seriously: 'None of the formal compliance reviews, ad-hoc reviews, site evaluations or audits FAS has conducted of Planet Aid projects have yielded any significant findings or concerns.'"

Reveal News did convince UNICEF, however, to cut ties with an organization that coordinates U.S. humanitarian programs in Malawi, following its investigations into DAPP (Development Aid from People to People). Funds intended for health and food projects were allegedly diverted elsewhere.

Some time after these articles appeared, Planet Aid filed a lawsuit against the Center for Investigative Reporting seeking a jury trial for "creating a false, misleading and defamatory image of" plaintiffs Planet Aid and DAPP Malawi country director Lisbeth Thomsen. Here are extracts from the legal complaint.

"This scheme also involved directly contacting individuals and groups and trying to convince them to stop doing business with Plaintiffs. The goal of this scheme was ultimately to drive Planet Aid out of business, and destroy Lisbeth Thomsen's reputation – all so that Defendants could falsely claim credit for having uncovered fraud, corruption and abuse in a government foreign aid program, and thereby attract additional donors to Defendants' news organization."

"More specifically, Defendants – along with a co-author who was a convicted felon in Malawi – published statements that Plaintiffs had engaged in 'systematic fraud,' 'stealing' and 'siphoning off of funds' from U.S. government relief programs, and "stripping" tens of millions of dollars from employee salaries. When they published those statements, Defendants knew, or were reckless in not knowing, that they were contrary to documents in their possession and information known by the same 'sources' they had interviewed. Defendants published statements about Plaintiffs even though some sources had flatly told Defendants that what they were publishing was not true."

"Other statements were elicited using various unlawful and improper tactics. Defendants Smith and Walters, for instance, impersonated U.S. governmental employees and others in an effort to convince individuals that Plaintiffs had cheated them, and had not provided them with all of the benefits to which they were entitled under the USDA program so that they would make false allegations against Plaintiffs. Further, as part of the scheme, Plaintiffs, either directly or through their agent and co-author, offered bribes and inducements to those who would assist in this scheme by similarly providing false and misleading information."

As of this writing, no trial date had been set. I wrote to CIR reporters about their stories and Planet Aid allegations against them, and asked as well what they thought of the corporations that fund them. I did not receive a reply.

Humana People-to-People Fundraising

Planet Aid is registered in Massachusetts and has its headquarters in Elkridge Maryland. It writes: "Marie Lichtenberg is a seasoned development professional with more than 26 years of global experience, having grown up in Zimbabwe and worked across Africa, Latin America and Asia. In her current position as the Director for International Partnerships for Planet Aid, she works closely with Planet Aid's sister organizations operating across Africa, India and Central America."
https://www.linkedin.com/in/marie-lichtenberg-5382a119

Through her efforts, HPP donated between $100,000 and $250,000 each year 2012, 2013, 2014 to the Clinton Foundation. The specific donation is not recorded, but the total sum would be between $300,000 and $750,000. HPP is therewith in the same donor category alongside major war criminal corporations such as Lockheed Martin, the world's largest war weaponry company, which sells F-35s to US and Denmark, among other warring nations. Other donors are Wall Street white-collar criminals: such as Lehman Brothers and JP Morgan Banks. Morgan was one of many big businesses that tried to "regime change" Franklin D. Roosevelt in 1933-4. This so-called "Business Plot" was exposed by Marine General Smedley Butler. *(See Note 1 at end of this chapter.)*
https://www.clintonfoundation.org/contributors?category=%24100%2C001%20to%20%24250%2C000&page=3

Sounds odd that an organization seeking donations for "fighting poverty with the poor" should be *giving* money to a corporation founded by a president and secretary of state, who are also lifelong attorneys for big capital. The strategy is clever enough when reading what fundraisers wrote: "Clinton Global Initiative will contribute by providing access to selected private

partners and wealthy individuals that are members of CGI. This is already happening."
https://www.documentcloud.org/documents/2800732-DNS-M3-S-Master-Plan-for-DNS-Global-Oct-28-2012-Ml.html#document

HPP fundraiser Marie Lichtenberg also helps Clintons' image by being a speaker for their foundation:
https://www.clintonfoundation.org/clinton-global-initiative/meetings/cgi-week-of-action/agenda/day-2

In return for her prestige and HPP donations, the Clintons advertise for HPP projects.
https://www.clintonfoundation.org/clinton-global-initiative/commitments/improving-food-security-and-farmer-income-malawi

Clinton Foundation is a private concern, although it benefits heavily from once having its founders in the White House. Maybe there is a connection here with the fact that the government founded US AID, which also donates to HPP projects. *(See Note 2 at end of this chapter.)*

HPP partners are listed in its literature: **US AID, European Commission, Centers for Disease Control and Prevention, US Department of Agriculture, The World Bank, Caribbean Development Bank**.

Except for the health control center, the others are major institutions of capitalism and some of them are actors for imperialism, especially US AID. I wrote to the Federation Humana People to People headquarters about its thoughts on why it was cooperating with such entities as US AID and the Clinton Foundation, receiving moneys and donating monies. I received two replies to two letters from Bolette Strandbygaard, a senior federation officer.

"In order to support these [international development] programmes, the members receive donor funding. When we commence funding for a new programme, we ensure that the organization funding this is informed of the goals of the programme, which are always in accordance with our values and commitment to international development..."

"Companies support Humana People to People members because they share some of the values that characterize the movement as quoted above, and because they believe that a Humana People to People project can help them fulfill their objectives, e.g. within social responsibility.

"The key factor for us in raising funds is that we generate enough income to carry out our work and implement long-term social development activities, and that those from whom we accept donations share our goals and vision to tackle major humanitarian and development challenges."

What is US AID all about?

Started in 1961, "U.S. foreign assistance has always had the twofold purpose of furthering America's interests while improving lives in the developing world. USAID carries out U.S. foreign policy by promoting broad-scale human progress at the same time it expands stable, free societies, creates markets and trade partners for the United States, and fosters good will abroad."

"USAID is the world's premier international development agency and a catalytic actor driving development results. USAID's work advances U.S. national security and economic prosperity, demonstrates American generosity, and promotes a path to recipient self-reliance and resilience."

"USAID is identifying new and innovative ways for corporate entities, non-governmental organizations, and individuals to partner with us in order to help countries on their development journey to self-reliance." https://www.usaid.gov/

"As good neighbors and supporters of the Venezuelan people, we are glad to be able to help, but we all know that this action is merely a short-term response, not a solution. For the sake of the Venezuelan people and the entire region, we must hope that the Maduro regime releases its crushing grip and that we see a return to democracy and to rule of law, for the sake of the Venezuelan people who deserve a peaceful, hopeful future." – Administrator Green https://www.usaid.gov/EstamosUnidosVE

Does that sound like "solidarity humanism" or the US Military Empire, responsible for over 500 aggressive wars in two and one-half centuries?

Marie Lichtenberg

In addition to Lichtenberg's relationship with the Clintons and US AID, she also supports Agfund.

"Arab Gulf Programme for Development (**AGFUND**) is a regional organization, established in 1980 by the initiative of His Royal Highness the late Prince Talal bin Abdulaziz and the support of the leaders of the Gulf Cooperation Council. AGFUND aims at the roots of human development problems, targeting all segments of society without discrimination." http://agfund.org/

Gulf Cooperation Council is a regional intergovernmental political and economic union consisting of all Arab states of the Persian Gulf except Iraq: Saudi Arabia, Bahrain, Kuwait, Oman, Qatar, and the United Arab Emirates.

The founder and president, Talal Bin Abdul Aziz al Saud, died in 2018. He was not an advocate of Saudi Arabia's absolute monarchy rather opted for a constitutional monarchy. In that extremely authoritarian-totalitarian Gulf state world, he was certainly a liberal, even known as the "red prince" for his reformist thinking. Still it seems quite contradictory that a leading member of the Teachers Group and Planet Aid's director of international partnerships would lend her name (and thereby HPP reputation) as a speaker for the monarchy capitalist organization. Below is what Agfund has on its website about *Marie Lichtenberg, Director of International Partnerships.*

Marie Lichtenberg

Marie Lichtenberg has over 27 years of global development experience. Most of her career has involved working for the Humana People to People Federation. She joined the Planet Aid office in Elkridge in 2011. Marie is responsible for mobilizing cooperative action among local, national, and international organizations, government agencies and business partners.

https://www.planetaid.org/about/leadership
https://agfundforum.org/ms-marie-lichtenberg/

I wrote to Marie Lichtenberg about her support for Agfund, the Clintons and USAID. How could she justify the values of HPP/Teachers Group and those of these institutions. She did not reply.

#

Note 1: Henry Ford and General Motors supplied the Nazi Wehrmact with a variety of thousands of vehicles for its wars. GM's overseas chief James Mooney received the Nazis "Order of the German Eagle", in 1938. Hitler's diplomats also gave Ford the "Grand Cross of the German Eagle" on Ford's 75th birthday, July 30, 1938. Hitler said of Ford, "I regard Henry Ford as my inspiration." (See my book, "The Russian Peace Threat: Pentagon on Alert", chapter 8.)

Note 2: In foreign policy, the Clintons were among the worst of warmongers. As president and secretary of state, they sent their warriors to murder people in Somalia, Rwanda, Haiti, Bosnia, Herzegovina, Yugoslavia, Afghanistan and Iraq. President Clinton's secretary of state and UN ambassador, Madeleine Albright, told CBS news that murdering half-a-million children from US bombings and economic-health sanctions was "worth it".

CONCLUSION

All organizations have warts. If it were not, however, for the deluge of malevolence that The Establishment pour onto Tvind/Teachers Group I might not feel obliged to write about their warts, except for one. That one, some of its fundraising practices, have I taken up in the last piece. In conclusion, I will expand a bit on that, take up a couple more infelicities, and share my authentic enthusiasm for most of what they do, for what I have seen.

In the three weeks I spent at their main schools in Denmark, at Tvind and Lindersvold, I must have spoken with a hundred teachers, administrators, and students. I also interviewed a dozen of them. I was with them in the kitchens, gardens, classrooms, sports centers and meeting halls. I found them, nearly all, to be open, friendly, thoughtful, intelligent, extremely hard-working, perhaps too much so for their own health in the long run. Some were not so forthcoming. They were, perhaps, marked by the deluge of malevolence—understandably so.

When I was with these anti-capitalist fighters against poverty, I was inspired and encouraged. They and their works warmed my heart. My heart even beat with joy sometimes whereas in my ordinary daily life, with the exception of warmth from my companion, Jette, I feel cold. My heart thumps with the pain that capitalism and its imperialist warring branches create. Watching their TV news, listening to their radio news, reading their newspapers cuts into my nerves, causing me to rage.

I exist betwixt the United States Military Empire and the Banana Kingdom Denmark. They lie to us constantly. Most of what the latter says about Tvind/TG are lies. They cannot even make juries and some judges believe their lies. Yet is "Amdi" a cult leader? I do not know really, and I don't think it matters that much if the alleged choir wanted it to be that way. He certainly could not be the Jim Jones or Al Capone that adversaries have named him. There are no charges of murder.

Since most of those who read my words are leftists, some communists of one stripe or another, I will remind you that many leftists-communists have made their own cults, especially those under the thumb of Comrade Stalin and Chairman Mao.

The Danes, nearly all of them whatever their politics, have cults, too: Vikings, Church of Martin Luther, and Queen Margrethe. Denmark is not even a banana republic because it is not a republic. It is a three-branch kingdom-state-church entity. Their church is the only one in the world recognized as the nation's church and named after a human being. And Martin

Luther was a racist and murderer. He hated and discriminated against Jews, he backed up princely landlords massacring poor peasants who wanted a better share of their labor, and he encouraged the burning alive of feminist women who he felt threatened by.

Do not the capitalists also practice cultism—their cult of the Yankee Dollar, of consumerism as a must in life? No, they don't have a one-person cult. Wall Street is their cult God. Wall Street is their dictator; the Pentagon and Langley their muscle to keep the billions of us peasants in our place. Those who defy that dictatorship are simply tortured and murdered. Tvind/Teachers Group do not do that. Have HPP project leaders in some places in the world skimmed from the till? A couple people that I know of have been punished for that charge, and there are probably more. I do know that such practice is the daily existence for practically every banker in the capitalist world. (See my previous piece, Fighting Capitalism with Capitalism.)

Ethics-Morality

Having said and meant the above, I turn to my main complaint about a handful of people in the Teachers Group who are in charge of raising funds for Humana People to People. Limits, there must be limits else what morality do we adhere to? How can we convince others that our path toward a truly liberated humane world society is any better than our enemies' path? Without morality, we remain alienated regardless of who is in charge.

How to define ethics-morality? That is a difficult question to answer, and even more difficult to reach agreement among large numbers of people and cultures. As I view it, morality is rules we apply to live by in order to be ethical. Ethical is being good with one another, caring for one another also those we cannot touch; living in harmony, in peace, in fellowship. To do that, we must share what we make, share natural resources, assure that the planet breathes life and not chemical death. It is immoral to steal from others, to make systems that favor some and exploit and destroy others, that require war-making, that destroy other life forms, the very planet itself. That is what capitalism does, that is what its imperialist arm does—that is what the United States Military Empire and its nearest allies, like Banana Kingdom Denmark are all about.

So that means that the ends do not justify the means, and that there must be limits to our actions, to our fundraising even when the end goal is good. If the means are bad, the goal ends up dirtied.

Teachers Group has set at least two limits to which I am aware: 1. No stock ownership. 2. No support to Monsanto. When some HPP project advertised for Monsanto seeds on a website, TG had it taken off. Monsanto steals from farmers, and forces them to use only sterilized seeds—GMO killer seeds. Ending up impoverished, more than one hundred thousand small farmers have committed suicide, especially in India. Monsanto is also a torturous murderer, making and selling agent orange, napalm and other horrendous chemical weapons, plus Roundup. https://www.globalresearch.ca/the-complete-history-of-monsanto-the-worlds-most-evil-corporation/5387964

What Monsanto does is just one small part of what USAID stands for being part of the "national security". To allegedly protect the "national security" US governments have conducted at least 535 wars and tens of thousands of minor military interventions. The numbers of human beings Denmark's Big Daddy has murdered in these "adventures" number in the scores of millions. (See my book, "The Russian Peace Threat: Pentagon on Alert" chapter 18. Herein are several links to researchers on this subject, including former CIA and military intelligence officers. In 2013, WIN/Galllup conducted a poll-survey of 66,000 people in 65 countries concerning world peace and threats. The greatest number found that "The United States is the Greatest Threat to World Peace".) https://nypost.com/2014/01/05/us-is-the-greatest-threat-to-world-peace-poll/)

I know that some Teacher Group members feel there should be more standardization with communications and marketing. With 3000 members spread over 45 countries, it is a difficult task. I say, it is worth it. So, do it again. Stop giving money to and taking money from the worst of the murdering capitalist institutions such as US AID and corporations like the Clintons. Run your own businesses, as Marie's brother Simon does. Give profits to your projects. If that means fewer projects so be it. Future revolutionaries, yourselves included, will be better morally recognized to help create the non-alienated "new man", "new woman" needed for true equality and peace.

The End

Headmaster, teacher, farmer Birthe raises worker's fist at day's end.

The Russian Peace Threat:
Pentagon on Alert

The Russian Peace Threat: Pentagon on Alert, a true historical page-turner, is destined to endure and inform future readers, writers and researchers about both what has been reported and what truly took place in the one hundred years from the 1917 Russian Revolution until the eruption of the distinct harbingers of the collapse of the US empire in the early twenty-first century.

Scandinavia on the Skids:
The Failure of Social Democracy

There is a good deal of misunderstanding what socialism and social democracy truly are. This book corrects these misunderstandings, and points to a direction that would eliminate poverty and inequality, which are the inevitable products free market globalization.

Yankee Sandinistas

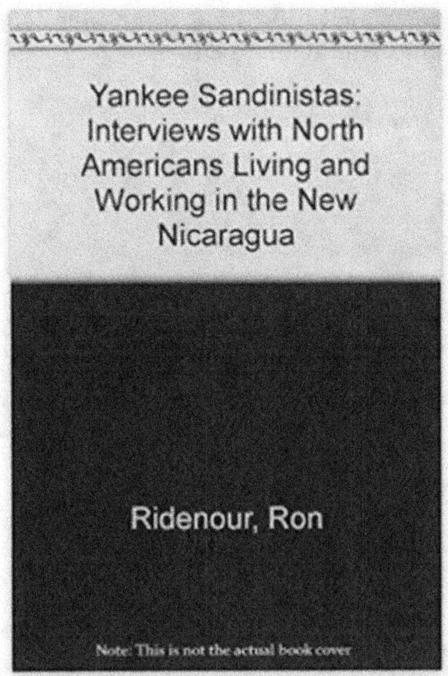

Graham Greene: Yankee Sandinistas "I found excellent and your publishers if they want to can quote me. I have marked nearly a dozen passages as is my habit when I am enjoying a book."

Ernesto Cardenal: "This book...is about (USs) savage war against our tiny country (while) Nicaraguans and North Americans join together and love each other more...for this reason (this book) has an historical importance--and touches the heart as well." [Cardenal is a Nicaraguan priest who was minister of culture during the first Sandinistas government from 1979.]

Philip Agee: "This book breaks through the cloud of atrocious lies...put forth daily to discredit and isolate the revolution. Northamericans can learn from this book...As a former volunteer coffee picker I say with pride that I'm a Yankee Sandinista too."

Noam Chomsky: "The decent, courageous and honorable people who speak here express in their words and lives the values we profess to hold, but that our government has long been dedicated to destroy. Perhaps they will help their fellow-citizens come to understand this central truth of modern history and to act to change it."

Back Fire: The CIA's Biggest Burn

Backfire is the first book written about the 26 Cuban and one Italian moles, who infiltrated the CIA for Cuba's Department of State Security, and came out in unision in 1987. The 50,000 book presents testimonies of three of the double agents, including the dean, who led a triple life for 21 years, a summary of the others, revels some of the major crimes and covert action efforts of the Agency, and elucidates the collaborative role the US mass media plays for the covert warriors. Cuba's counterintelligence proves that the CIA never stopped attempting to murder Fidel Castro nor did it give up the vain hope of destroying the Cuban socialist revolution despite U.S. congressional investigations of CIA terrorist activities.

About Ron Ridenour

Ron Ridenour was born in the US Military Empire, 1939. After four years in the Air Force, he rejected the American Dream, in 1961, and has since acted as an anti-war, anti-racist and solidarity radical activist (Long Hot Summer, 1964, in Mississippi; Wounded Knee AIM 1973; anti-Vietnam war coordinator in Los Angeles). He has lived in many countries and worked as a journalist-editor-author-translator for five decades, including for Cuba's Editorial José Martí and Prensa Latina (1988-96). He has lived in Denmark for three decades agitating against its vassal state mentality and warmongering.

Photo by Sandra

Legal Notices and Disclaimers

Winding Brook Stories is an original work by Ron Ridenour protected under international copyright law © Ron Ridenour 2019.

All rights to this work are reserved. Without limiting the rights under copyright reserved above, no part of this publication may be reproduced, stored in or introduced into a retrieval system, archived, or transmitted, in any form, or by any means (electronic, mechanical, photocopying, recording, or otherwise) without the prior written permission of the copyright owner of this book.

The author acknowledges the trademarked status and trademark owners of any products referenced in this work, which have been used without permission. The publication/use of these trademarks is not authorized, associated with, or sponsored by the trademark owners, but appear as common and casual references in the context of presenting ideas, as such trademarked entities are common features in modern everyday life. No product endorsements are meant or implied by their use.

www.ingramcontent.com/pod-product-compliance
Lightning Source LLC
Chambersburg PA
CBHW061350250726
48657CB00004B/1428